# INTIMACY UNVEILED: EXPLORING THE DEPTHS OF HUMAN CONNECTION

# AUTHOR: RAJ KISHOR MAHAPATRA

@itsrkmahapatra

---

# DISCLAIMER

The content presented in this book is for informational purposes only and reflects the author's opinions and experiences. While every effort has been made to ensure the accuracy and reliability of the information provided, the author assumes no responsibility for errors, omissions, or discrepancies. Readers are encouraged to consult professional advice for specific personal or medical issues related to intimacy. The book is intended for mature audiences and discusses topics that may not be suitable for younger readers.

# DESCRIPTION

"Intimacy Unveiled: Exploring the Depths of Human Connection" delves into the complex and multifaceted nature of intimacy, a fundamental aspect of human relationships. From emotional bonding to physical closeness, this book provides a comprehensive exploration of how intimacy shapes our lives and enhances our connections with others.

With over 50 insightful chapters, Raj Kishor Mahapatra takes readers on a journey through the different dimensions of intimacy, offering practical advice, real-world examples, and inspiring stories. This book aims to help readers understand and cultivate intimacy in their relationships, promoting healthier, more fulfilling connections with loved ones.

## Table of Contents

# CHAPTER 1: INTRODUCTION TO INTIMACY

Intimacy is an essential component of human relationships, encompassing emotional, physical, and psychological closeness between individuals. It goes beyond mere physical attraction, involving a deep connection that fosters trust, understanding, and mutual respect. This chapter introduces the concept of intimacy, highlighting its importance in various types of relationships and setting the stage for the comprehensive exploration that follows.

# CHAPTER 2: THE IMPORTANCE OF EMOTIONAL INTIMACY

Emotional intimacy involves sharing thoughts, feelings, and experiences with another person, creating a strong bond based on mutual understanding and trust. This chapter delves into the significance of emotional intimacy, discussing how it enhances relationships and contributes to overall well-being.

# CHAPTER 3: PHYSICAL INTIMACY: BEYOND THE SURFACE

Physical intimacy is often associated with sexual activity, but it also includes non-sexual touch, such as hugging, holding hands, and cuddling. This chapter explores the different aspects of physical intimacy and its role in strengthening relationships.

# CHAPTER 4: BUILDING TRUST IN RELATIONSHIPS

Trust is a cornerstone of intimacy, allowing individuals to feel safe and secure in their relationships. This chapter examines the process of building and maintaining trust, addressing common challenges and offering practical tips for fostering a trusting environment.

# CHAPTER 5: COMMUNICATION: THE KEY TO INTIMACY

Effective communication is crucial for developing and sustaining intimacy. This chapter provides insights into the importance of open and honest communication, offering strategies for improving communication skills and resolving conflicts.

# CHAPTER 6: INTIMACY IN FRIENDSHIPS

Intimacy is not limited to romantic relationships; it is also a vital component of close friendships. This chapter discusses the unique aspects of intimacy in friendships, highlighting the importance of emotional support and shared experiences.

# CHAPTER 7: ROMANTIC INTIMACY: A DEEP DIVE

Romantic intimacy involves a combination of emotional, physical, and sexual closeness. This chapter explores the complexities of romantic intimacy, offering advice on how to cultivate and maintain a deep, loving connection with a partner.

# CHAPTER 8: INTIMACY IN MARRIAGE

Marriage is often considered the ultimate expression of romantic intimacy. This chapter examines the dynamics of intimacy within marriage, addressing common challenges and providing practical tips for nurturing a strong, intimate bond.

# CHAPTER 9: INTIMACY AND VULNERABILITY

Vulnerability is an integral part of intimacy, allowing individuals to share their true selves without fear of judgment. This chapter explores the role of vulnerability in fostering deep connections and offers guidance on how to embrace vulnerability in relationships.

# CHAPTER 10: OVERCOMING BARRIERS TO INTIMACY

Various factors can hinder intimacy, including past traumas, communication issues, and personal insecurities. This chapter identifies common barriers to intimacy and provides strategies for overcoming them.

# CHAPTER 11: THE ROLE OF EMPATHY

Empathy is the ability to understand and share the feelings of another person. This chapter discusses the importance of empathy in building intimate connections and offers tips for developing empathetic skills.

# CHAPTER 12: SEXUAL INTIMACY: MYTHS AND REALITIES

Sexual intimacy is a vital aspect of many relationships, but it is often surrounded by myths and misconceptions. This chapter addresses common myths about sexual intimacy and provides a realistic perspective on its role in relationships.

# CHAPTER 13: THE POWER OF NON-SEXUAL TOUCH

Non-sexual touch, such as hugging, holding hands, and cuddling, plays a significant role in fostering intimacy. This chapter explores the benefits of non-sexual touch and its impact on relationship satisfaction.

# CHAPTER 14: INTIMACY IN LONG-DISTANCE RELATIONSHIPS

Maintaining intimacy in long-distance relationships can be challenging, but it is possible with effort and commitment. This chapter offers practical advice for sustaining intimacy across distances.

# CHAPTER 15: CULTURAL PERSPECTIVES ON INTIMACY

Intimacy is influenced by cultural norms and values. This chapter examines how different cultures perceive and express intimacy, highlighting the diversity of intimate practices around the world.

# CHAPTER 16: TECHNOLOGY AND INTIMACY

Technology has transformed the way we connect with others, impacting intimacy in various ways. This chapter explores the effects of technology on intimacy, discussing both its benefits and potential drawbacks.

# CHAPTER 17: INTIMACY IN THE DIGITAL AGE

The digital age has brought new opportunities and challenges for intimate relationships. This chapter delves into the impact of social media, online dating, and virtual communication on intimacy.

# CHAPTER 18: THE IMPACT OF SOCIAL MEDIA

Social media can both enhance and hinder intimacy. This chapter examines the role of social media in relationships, offering tips for balancing online interactions with face-to-face connections.

# CHAPTER 19: INTIMACY AND MENTAL HEALTH

Intimacy is closely linked to mental health, with positive relationships contributing to emotional well-being. This chapter discusses the connection between intimacy and mental health, highlighting the benefits of intimate connections for psychological resilience.

# CHAPTER 20: REBUILDING INTIMACY AFTER CONFLICT

Conflicts are inevitable in relationships, but they can also provide opportunities for growth and deeper intimacy. This chapter offers strategies for rebuilding intimacy after conflicts, focusing on forgiveness, communication, and mutual understanding.

# CHAPTER 21: INTIMACY IN PARENTHOOD

Parenthood brings new challenges and opportunities for intimacy. This chapter explores how becoming parents affects intimacy between partners and offers tips for maintaining a strong connection amidst the demands of parenting.

# CHAPTER 22: INTIMACY IN LATER LIFE

Intimacy continues to play a vital role in relationships as people age. This chapter examines the unique aspects of intimacy in later life, discussing the challenges and opportunities for older adults to maintain intimate connections.

# CHAPTER 23: INTIMACY AND SELF-DISCOVERY

Understanding oneself is crucial for developing intimate relationships with others. This chapter explores the journey of self-discovery and its impact on intimacy, offering insights into how personal growth enhances relational connections.

# CHAPTER 24: MINDFULNESS AND INTIMACY

Mindfulness involves being present and fully engaged in the moment, which can enhance intimacy. This chapter discusses the benefits of mindfulness for intimacy and provides practical exercises for cultivating mindfulness in relationships.

# CHAPTER 25: THE SCIENCE OF INTIMACY

Intimacy has been studied extensively by researchers, revealing fascinating insights into its nature and effects. This chapter delves into the scientific understanding of intimacy, discussing key findings from psychological and physiological research.

# CHAPTER 26: INTIMACY IN LGBTQ + RELATIONSHIPS

Intimacy in LGBTQ+ relationships may face unique challenges and dynamics. This chapter explores the experiences of LGBTQ + individuals in intimate relationships, highlighting the importance of acceptance and understanding.

# CHAPTER 27: OVERCOMING INTIMACY ISSUES

Many people face challenges in developing and maintaining intimacy. This chapter identifies common intimacy issues and provides strategies for addressing them, focusing on communication, empathy, and self-awareness.

# CHAPTER 28: THE ROLE OF THERAPY

Therapy can be a valuable resource for individuals and couples seeking to improve their intimate relationships. This chapter discusses the role of therapy in fostering intimacy, highlighting different therapeutic approaches and their benefits.

# CHAPTER 29: INTIMACY AND PERSONAL BOUNDARIES

Establishing and respecting personal boundaries is crucial for healthy intimacy. This chapter explores the importance of boundaries in relationships, offering guidance on how to communicate and uphold them effectively.

# CHAPTER 30: THE LANGUAGE OF LOVE

Understanding and expressing love in different ways is essential for intimacy. This chapter delves into the concept of love languages, discussing how individuals can identify and communicate their love languages to enhance intimacy.

# CHAPTER 31: INTIMACY IN CRISIS SITUATIONS

Crises can strain intimate relationships but can also bring people closer together. This chapter examines how to maintain and strengthen intimacy during difficult times, offering strategies for coping and supporting each other.

# CHAPTER 32: INTIMACY IN TIMES OF CHANGE

Life changes, such as moving, career transitions, and health issues, can impact intimacy. This chapter discusses how to navigate changes while maintaining intimate connections, emphasizing flexibility and communication.

# CHAPTER 33: SPIRITUAL INTIMACY

Spiritual intimacy involves sharing beliefs, values, and practices with another person. This chapter explores the role of spirituality in fostering deep connections and offers tips for cultivating spiritual intimacy.

# CHAPTER 34: INTIMACY AND CREATIVITY

Creativity can enhance intimacy by providing new ways to connect and express emotions. This chapter discusses the relationship between intimacy and creativity, offering suggestions for incorporating creative activities into relationships.

# CHAPTER 35: DEVELOPING INTIMACY SKILLS

Intimacy skills can be learned and developed over time. This chapter provides practical exercises and techniques for enhancing intimacy, focusing on communication, empathy, and emotional expression.

# CHAPTER 36: THE INFLUENCE OF FAMILY DYNAMICS

Family dynamics play a significant role in shaping individuals' understanding and experience of intimacy. This chapter examines the impact of family relationships on intimacy and offers insights into overcoming familial challenges.

# CHAPTER 37: INTIMACY IN THE WORKPLACE

Workplace relationships can involve varying degrees of intimacy, from professional camaraderie to deeper connections. This chapter discusses the nuances of intimacy in the workplace, highlighting the importance of boundaries and professionalism.

# CHAPTER 38: BALANCING INTIMACY AND INDEPENDENCE

Maintaining a balance between intimacy and independence is crucial for healthy relationships. This chapter explores how individuals can nurture intimate connections while preserving their autonomy and personal identity.

# CHAPTER 39: INTIMACY AND PERSONAL GROWTH

Personal growth and self-improvement can enhance intimacy by fostering self-awareness and emotional intelligence. This chapter discusses the interplay between personal development and intimate relationships, offering tips for integrating growth into relational dynamics.

# CHAPTER 40: INTIMACY IN CASUAL RELATIONSHIPS

Casual relationships can involve varying levels of intimacy, depending on the individuals' preferences and expectations. This chapter explores the nature of intimacy in casual relationships, discussing how to navigate boundaries and communication.

# CHAPTER 41: THE ROLE OF PLAYFULNESS

Playfulness can enhance intimacy by bringing joy, spontaneity, and connection to relationships. This chapter discusses the benefits of playfulness for intimacy and offers suggestions for incorporating play into relationships.

# CHAPTER 42: INTIMACY IN ADVERSITY

Adversity can challenge intimate relationships, but it can also strengthen bonds through shared resilience. This chapter examines how to maintain and deepen intimacy during challenging times, emphasizing support and mutual understanding.

# CHAPTER 43: THE FUTURE OF INTIMACY

As society evolves, so do the dynamics of intimacy. This chapter explores emerging trends and potential future developments in intimate relationships, considering the impact of technology, social changes, and cultural shifts.

# CHAPTER 44: NURTURING INTIMACY IN DAILY LIFE

Intimacy is built through everyday interactions and experiences. This chapter offers practical tips for nurturing intimacy in daily life, focusing on small gestures, quality time, and consistent communication.

# CHAPTER 45: THE IMPACT OF TRAUMA ON INTIMACY

Trauma can significantly impact an individual's ability to develop and maintain intimate relationships. This chapter discusses the effects of trauma on intimacy and provides strategies for healing and rebuilding trust.

# CHAPTER 46: HEALING AND REBUILDING INTIMACY

Healing from past wounds is essential for fostering intimacy. This chapter explores the process of healing and rebuilding intimacy, offering guidance on how to move forward and create healthier connections.

# CHAPTER 47: INTIMACY AND ETHICAL NON-MONOGAMY

Ethical non-monogamy involves consensual and transparent relationships with multiple partners. This chapter examines the dynamics of intimacy in non-monogamous relationships, highlighting the importance of communication and trust.

# CHAPTER 48: EXPLORING SENSUAL INTIMACY

Sensual intimacy involves engaging the senses to enhance connection and pleasure. This chapter explores the role of sensuality in intimate relationships, offering tips for deepening sensual connections.

# CHAPTER 49: THE JOURNEY OF LIFELONG INTIMACY

Lifelong intimacy requires ongoing effort and commitment. This chapter discusses the journey of maintaining intimacy over the long term, emphasizing the importance of adaptability, communication, and mutual support.

# CHAPTER 50: CONCLUSION: EMBRACING INTIMACY

The final chapter summarizes the key insights from the book, encouraging readers to embrace intimacy in all its forms. It emphasizes the value of intimate connections for personal growth, emotional well-being, and overall life satisfaction.

---

"Intimacy Unveiled: Exploring the Depths of Human Connection" aims to be a comprehensive guide for readers seeking to understand and enhance intimacy in their lives. By offering a blend of practical advice, scientific insights, and real-world examples, this book provides valuable tools for cultivating deep and meaningful relationships.

# CHAPTER 1: INTRODUCTION TO INTIMACY

Intimacy is an essential component of human relationships, encompassing emotional, physical, and psychological closeness between individuals. It goes beyond mere physical attraction, involving a deep connection that fosters trust, understanding, and mutual respect. This chapter introduces the concept of intimacy, highlighting its importance in various types of relationships and setting the stage for the comprehensive exploration that follows.

**The Essence of Intimacy**

Intimacy is the glue that binds individuals together, creating a sense of belonging and connection. It is the profound feeling of being deeply known and understood by another person, allowing for the free expression of thoughts, emotions, and desires. This closeness is not limited to romantic relationships; it can be found in friendships, familial bonds, and even professional connections.

Intimacy involves several key elements:

1. **Emotional Closeness**: Sharing personal feelings, fears, and aspirations.

2. **Physical Closeness**: Engaging in physical touch and proximity.

3. **Psychological Closeness**: Understanding and

supporting each other's mental and emotional states.

These elements work together to create a comprehensive sense of intimacy that enhances our overall well-being and happiness.

## The Importance of Intimacy

Intimacy plays a crucial role in our lives, influencing our mental, emotional, and physical health. Here are some reasons why intimacy is important:

1. **Emotional Support**: Intimate relationships provide a strong support system, helping us navigate life's challenges and celebrate its joys.

2. **Mental Health**: Close connections can reduce stress, anxiety, and depression, contributing to better mental health.

3. **Physical Health**: Intimacy has been linked to improved physical health, including lower blood pressure, better immune function, and reduced risk of chronic diseases.

4. **Personal Growth**: Intimate relationships encourage personal growth by providing a safe space for self-expression and vulnerability.

## Types of Intimacy

Intimacy can take many forms, each contributing uniquely to our relationships. Some of the main types of intimacy include:

1. **Emotional Intimacy**: Involves sharing personal thoughts and feelings, fostering a deep emotional connection.

2. **Physical Intimacy**: Encompasses both sexual and non-sexual touch, such as hugging, kissing, and cuddling.

3. **Intellectual Intimacy**: Sharing ideas, engaging in

stimulating conversations, and appreciating each other's intellect.

4. **Experiential Intimacy**: Bonding through shared experiences and activities.

5. **Spiritual Intimacy**: Connecting on a spiritual level, sharing beliefs, values, and practices.

## Building Intimacy

Building intimacy requires effort, communication, and vulnerability. Here are some strategies to cultivate intimacy in your relationships:

1. **Open Communication**: Share your thoughts and feelings honestly and encourage your partner to do the same.

2. **Active Listening**: Listen attentively and empathetically, showing that you value and understand the other person's perspective.

3. **Quality Time**: Spend meaningful time together, engaging in activities that you both enjoy.

4. **Physical Affection**: Express affection through physical touch, whether it's a hug, a kiss, or holding hands.

5. **Mutual Support**: Be there for each other in times of need, offering emotional and practical support.

## Challenges to Intimacy

While intimacy is deeply rewarding, it can also be challenging to achieve and maintain. Common barriers to intimacy include:

1. **Fear of Vulnerability**: The fear of being judged or rejected can prevent people from opening up.

2. **Communication Issues**: Misunderstandings and lack of communication can hinder intimacy.

3. **Past Trauma**: Previous negative experiences can impact one's ability to trust and be intimate.

4. **Busy Lifestyles**: Lack of time and stress can make it difficult to prioritize intimacy.

## The Journey Ahead

This book aims to provide a comprehensive guide to understanding and enhancing intimacy in all aspects of life. In the chapters that follow, we will explore various dimensions of intimacy, from emotional and physical closeness to the role of technology and cultural perspectives. We will also address common challenges and offer practical strategies for building and maintaining intimate relationships.

By delving into the depths of human connection, we hope to empower readers to cultivate deeper, more meaningful relationships that enrich their lives and promote overall well-being. Intimacy is not a destination but a continuous journey of growth, understanding, and mutual respect. Let us embark on this journey together, exploring the many facets of intimacy and discovering the profound impact it can have on our lives.

In the next chapter, we will explore the importance of emotional intimacy, delving into how sharing personal feelings and experiences can strengthen our connections with others. We will discuss practical ways to foster emotional intimacy and overcome common barriers. Join us as we continue this journey into the heart of human connection.

# CHAPTER 2: THE IMPORTANCE OF EMOTIONAL INTIMACY

Emotional intimacy involves sharing thoughts, feelings, and experiences with another person, creating a strong bond based on mutual understanding and trust. This chapter delves into the significance of emotional intimacy, discussing how it enhances relationships and contributes to overall well-being.

**Defining Emotional Intimacy**

Emotional intimacy is the deep sense of closeness and connection that allows individuals to feel safe, understood, and supported. It goes beyond surface-level interactions, enabling people to share their innermost thoughts, fears, dreams, and vulnerabilities. Emotional intimacy is the foundation of strong, healthy relationships, fostering a sense of belonging and security.

**The Role of Emotional Intimacy in Relationships**

1. **Strengthening Bonds**: Emotional intimacy creates a strong bond between individuals, whether in romantic relationships, friendships, or familial ties. It helps build trust and loyalty, making the relationship more resilient to challenges.

2. **Enhancing Communication**: When people feel

emotionally close, they are more likely to communicate openly and honestly. This transparency fosters a deeper understanding and reduces misunderstandings.

3. **Promoting Empathy and Compassion**: Emotional intimacy allows individuals to empathize with each other's experiences and emotions, promoting compassion and support. This mutual empathy strengthens the connection and creates a nurturing environment.

4. **Building Trust**: Sharing personal thoughts and feelings requires vulnerability. When this vulnerability is met with acceptance and understanding, it builds trust and confidence in the relationship.

5. **Fostering Mutual Respect**: Emotional intimacy encourages mutual respect by recognizing and valuing each other's feelings and experiences. This respect forms the basis of a healthy and balanced relationship.

## Benefits of Emotional Intimacy

1. **Improved Mental Health**: Emotional intimacy provides emotional support, reducing feelings of loneliness, anxiety, and depression. It enhances overall mental health and well-being by creating a sense of connection and belonging.

2. **Increased Relationship Satisfaction**: Relationships with high levels of emotional intimacy are often more satisfying and fulfilling. This satisfaction comes from feeling valued, understood, and supported by the other person.

3. **Enhanced Conflict Resolution**: Emotional intimacy improves the ability to resolve conflicts

constructively. When individuals feel emotionally connected, they are more likely to approach conflicts with empathy, understanding, and a willingness to find solutions.

4. **Greater Life Satisfaction**: The positive impact of emotional intimacy extends beyond individual relationships, contributing to overall life satisfaction. Feeling connected and supported enhances one's quality of life and overall happiness.

## Cultivating Emotional Intimacy

Building emotional intimacy requires intentional effort and communication. Here are some strategies to foster emotional intimacy in relationships:

1. **Open and Honest Communication**: Share your thoughts, feelings, and experiences openly with the other person. Encourage them to do the same, creating a safe space for vulnerability and authenticity.

2. **Active Listening**: Practice active listening by fully engaging with the other person's words and emotions. Show empathy and understanding, validating their feelings and experiences.

3. **Express Appreciation and Gratitude**: Regularly express appreciation and gratitude for the other person. Acknowledge their positive qualities, efforts, and contributions to the relationship.

4. **Spend Quality Time Together**: Make time for meaningful interactions and shared activities. Quality time strengthens the emotional connection and creates lasting memories.

5. **Show Empathy and Support**: Be empathetic and supportive during difficult times. Offer a listening ear, a comforting presence, and practical assistance

when needed.

6. **Share Personal Experiences**: Sharing personal experiences, both positive and negative, deepens the emotional bond. It allows individuals to connect on a deeper level and understand each other's unique journeys.

7. **Practice Vulnerability**: Embrace vulnerability by sharing your fears, insecurities, and dreams. Vulnerability fosters trust and creates a deeper emotional connection.

## Overcoming Barriers to Emotional Intimacy

Several factors can hinder the development of emotional intimacy. Recognizing and addressing these barriers is crucial for fostering deeper connections:

1. **Fear of Rejection**: The fear of being rejected or judged can prevent individuals from opening up emotionally. Overcoming this fear requires building trust and creating a safe, non-judgmental environment.

2. **Past Trauma**: Previous negative experiences or trauma can impact one's ability to develop emotional intimacy. Seeking professional support and engaging in healing practices can help overcome these barriers.

3. **Communication Issues**: Poor communication skills can hinder emotional intimacy. Improving communication through active listening, empathy, and assertiveness can enhance emotional connections.

4. **Lack of Time**: Busy lifestyles and demanding schedules can limit the time available for emotional bonding. Prioritizing quality time and making a conscious effort to connect can overcome this

barrier.

5. **Personal Insecurities**: Insecurities and low self-esteem can affect one's ability to be vulnerable and open. Building self-confidence and seeking support can help address these issues.

## Practical Exercises to Enhance Emotional Intimacy

Here are some practical exercises to help build and enhance emotional intimacy in relationships:

1. **Daily Check-Ins**: Set aside time each day to check in with each other. Share your thoughts, feelings, and experiences, and listen attentively to the other person.

2. **Emotional Sharing**: Regularly share your emotions with each other. Use "I feel" statements to express your feelings and encourage the other person to do the same.

3. **Deep Conversations**: Engage in deep and meaningful conversations about your values, dreams, and aspirations. Explore each other's perspectives and experiences.

4. **Active Listening Practice**: Practice active listening by focusing on the other person's words and emotions. Reflect back what you hear to show understanding and empathy.

5. **Gratitude Journaling**: Keep a gratitude journal and regularly share entries with each other. Express appreciation for the positive aspects of your relationship and the other person's contributions.

6. **Joint Activities**: Engage in activities that you both enjoy and that foster emotional bonding. Whether it's a hobby, a sport, or a creative project, shared activities create opportunities for connection.

7. **Mindfulness Practices**: Practice mindfulness together, focusing on the present moment and each other's presence. Mindfulness enhances emotional awareness and connection.

## Conclusion

Emotional intimacy is the foundation of strong, healthy relationships. It fosters trust, understanding, and mutual respect, enhancing communication, empathy, and overall well-being. By cultivating emotional intimacy, individuals can build deeper, more meaningful connections that enrich their lives and contribute to their overall happiness.

In the next chapter, we will explore the role of physical intimacy in relationships. We will discuss how physical closeness, both sexual and non-sexual, contributes to emotional bonding and overall relationship satisfaction. Join us as we continue to delve into the various dimensions of intimacy and their impact on our lives.

# CHAPTER 3: PHYSICAL INTIMACY: BEYOND THE SURFACE

Physical intimacy is often associated with sexual activity, but it also includes non-sexual touch, such as hugging, holding hands, and cuddling. This chapter explores the different aspects of physical intimacy and its role in strengthening relationships.

**Understanding Physical Intimacy**

Physical intimacy involves the physical expression of closeness and affection between individuals. It encompasses a range of behaviors, from casual gestures like a friendly pat on the back to more intimate acts like kissing and sexual intercourse. Physical intimacy is a powerful way to communicate love, care, and connection, transcending verbal communication.

**Types of Physical Intimacy**

1. **Non-Sexual Touch**: This includes gestures such as hugging, holding hands, cuddling, and kissing. Non-sexual touch is an essential component of physical intimacy, providing comfort, reassurance, and a sense of security.

2. **Sexual Intimacy**: This involves sexual activity and the expression of sexual desire and attraction.

Sexual intimacy is a significant aspect of romantic relationships, contributing to emotional bonding and overall relationship satisfaction.

3. **Affectionate Touch**: Simple acts of affection, such as a gentle touch on the arm, a peck on the cheek, or a warm embrace, play a crucial role in maintaining physical intimacy. These gestures express love and appreciation, reinforcing emotional closeness.

**The Importance of Physical Intimacy**

1. **Enhancing Emotional Connection**: Physical intimacy reinforces emotional bonds by creating a sense of closeness and security. It helps individuals feel valued, loved, and understood.

2. **Reducing Stress**: Physical touch has been shown to reduce stress levels by releasing oxytocin, a hormone associated with bonding and relaxation. This stress reduction promotes overall well-being and mental health.

3. **Improving Communication**: Physical intimacy enhances non-verbal communication, allowing individuals to express emotions and intentions through touch. This non-verbal communication can strengthen understanding and empathy.

4. **Promoting Relationship Satisfaction**: Physical intimacy contributes to relationship satisfaction by fulfilling the need for closeness and affection. It enhances feelings of love and commitment, fostering a deeper connection.

5. **Boosting Physical Health**: Physical touch has numerous health benefits, including lowering blood pressure, boosting the immune system, and reducing pain. These benefits contribute to overall physical health and well-being.

## Building and Maintaining Physical Intimacy

1. **Prioritize Touch**: Make physical touch a priority in your relationships. Simple gestures like hugging, holding hands, and cuddling can significantly enhance physical intimacy.

2. **Be Present**: Be fully present during moments of physical intimacy. Focus on the other person and the connection you are creating, rather than being distracted by external factors.

3. **Communicate Needs and Preferences**: Openly communicate your needs and preferences regarding physical touch. Discuss what types of touch you enjoy and how often you would like to engage in physical intimacy.

4. **Be Attentive to Boundaries**: Respect each other's boundaries and comfort levels. Ensure that physical touch is consensual and mutually enjoyable.

5. **Create Opportunities for Intimacy**: Find opportunities to engage in physical intimacy throughout the day. Whether it's a quick hug before work or a longer cuddle session in the evening, these moments build and maintain intimacy.

6. **Explore Different Types of Touch**: Experiment with different types of touch to discover what feels best for both partners. This exploration can enhance physical intimacy and make it more fulfilling.

7. **Maintain Physical Health**: Taking care of your physical health can enhance physical intimacy. Regular exercise, a healthy diet, and adequate rest contribute to your overall well-being and ability to engage in physical touch.

## Overcoming Barriers to Physical Intimacy

Several factors can hinder the development of physical

intimacy. Recognizing and addressing these barriers is crucial for fostering deeper connections:

1. **Busy Lifestyles**: Demanding schedules and busy lifestyles can limit opportunities for physical intimacy. Prioritizing time for touch and connection is essential.

2. **Stress and Fatigue**: High stress levels and fatigue can reduce the desire for physical intimacy. Managing stress through relaxation techniques and ensuring adequate rest can help.

3. **Body Image Issues**: Insecurities about one's body can affect the willingness to engage in physical intimacy. Building self-confidence and seeking support can help overcome these issues.

4. **Communication Barriers**: Poor communication can hinder physical intimacy. Improving communication skills and discussing needs and preferences can enhance the physical connection.

5. **Past Trauma**: Previous negative experiences or trauma can impact one's ability to engage in physical intimacy. Seeking professional support and engaging in healing practices can help address these barriers.

**Practical Exercises to Enhance Physical Intimacy**

Here are some practical exercises to help build and enhance physical intimacy in relationships:

1. **Daily Touch Rituals**: Establish daily touch rituals, such as a morning hug or a goodnight kiss. These rituals create consistent opportunities for physical connection.

2. **Massage Sessions**: Give each other massages to promote relaxation and physical closeness. Massages can be a soothing and intimate way to connect.

3. **Dance Together**: Dancing together, whether it's a slow dance or a more energetic one, can enhance physical intimacy and create joyful, shared experiences.

4. **Cuddle Time**: Set aside time for cuddling without distractions. Cuddling fosters physical closeness and emotional bonding.

5. **Holding Hands**: Hold hands while walking or sitting together. This simple gesture can strengthen the physical connection.

6. **Non-Sexual Touch**: Engage in non-sexual touch throughout the day, such as a gentle touch on the arm or a reassuring pat on the back. These gestures reinforce physical intimacy.

7. **Explore Sensual Touch**: Experiment with different types of touch, such as gentle caresses or playful tickling. Exploring sensual touch can enhance physical intimacy and create a deeper connection.

## Conclusion

Physical intimacy is a vital aspect of relationships, encompassing both sexual and non-sexual touch. It enhances emotional connection, reduces stress, and promotes overall well-being. By prioritizing touch, being present, and communicating openly, individuals can build and maintain physical intimacy, creating deeper and more fulfilling connections.

In the next chapter, we will explore the role of psychological intimacy in relationships. We will discuss how understanding and supporting each other's mental and emotional states contribute to a stronger bond and overall relationship satisfaction. Join us as we continue to delve into the various dimensions of intimacy and their impact on our lives.

# CHAPTER 4: BUILDING TRUST IN RELATIONSHIPS

Trust is a cornerstone of intimacy, allowing individuals to feel safe and secure in their relationships. This chapter examines the process of building and maintaining trust, addressing common challenges, and offering practical tips for fostering a trusting environment.

## Understanding Trust

Trust is the belief in the reliability, truth, ability, or strength of someone or something. In relationships, trust involves feeling confident that the other person will act in your best interest, keep their promises, and be dependable. Trust is essential for emotional, physical, and psychological intimacy, as it provides a foundation of security and safety.

## The Role of Trust in Intimacy

1. **Emotional Safety**: Trust creates a safe space for individuals to express their thoughts, feelings, and vulnerabilities without fear of judgment or rejection. This emotional safety is crucial for developing emotional intimacy.

2. **Reliability and Dependability**: Trust ensures that partners can rely on each other to keep promises and be there when needed. This reliability strengthens the bond and fosters a sense of security.

3. **Open Communication**: Trust encourages open and honest communication. When trust is present, individuals feel comfortable sharing their true selves, leading to deeper connections.

4. **Conflict Resolution**: Trust facilitates effective conflict resolution. When partners trust each other's intentions, they can address disagreements with empathy and understanding, rather than suspicion and defensiveness.

5. **Mutual Respect**: Trust fosters mutual respect by acknowledging each other's integrity and reliability. This respect forms the basis of a healthy and balanced relationship.

## Building Trust in Relationships

1. **Consistent Honesty**: Being honest and transparent in all interactions is fundamental to building trust. Consistency in truthfulness creates a foundation of reliability and dependability.

2. **Keep Promises**: Follow through on commitments and promises. Keeping your word, no matter how small the promise, reinforces reliability and strengthens trust.

3. **Open Communication**: Encourage open and honest communication. Share your thoughts, feelings, and concerns, and listen actively to your partner's perspectives.

4. **Be Dependable**: Show up and be there for your partner in times of need. Dependability demonstrates that you can be relied upon, building confidence in the relationship.

5. **Respect Boundaries**: Respect each other's boundaries and personal space. Acknowledging and honoring boundaries fosters a sense of safety and

trust.

6. **Apologize and Forgive**: When mistakes are made, offer sincere apologies and seek forgiveness. Similarly, be willing to forgive and let go of grudges. Apologizing and forgiving reinforce trust by showing accountability and empathy.

7. **Be Vulnerable**: Share your vulnerabilities and encourage your partner to do the same. Vulnerability fosters intimacy and trust by creating a deeper emotional connection.

## Maintaining Trust

Building trust is an ongoing process that requires continuous effort and commitment. Here are some strategies to maintain trust in relationships:

1. **Consistent Behavior**: Maintain consistency in your actions and words. Predictable and consistent behavior reinforces trust and reliability.

2. **Regular Check-Ins**: Regularly check in with your partner about the state of your relationship. Discuss any concerns or issues that may arise and address them proactively.

3. **Show Appreciation**: Regularly express appreciation for your partner's efforts and contributions to the relationship. Acknowledging each other's positive actions reinforces trust and mutual respect.

4. **Practice Empathy**: Show empathy and understanding during difficult times. Being empathetic demonstrates that you value and support your partner, strengthening the bond of trust.

5. **Avoid Secrets**: Avoid keeping secrets that could harm the relationship. Transparency and openness are essential for maintaining trust.

6. **Be Reliable**: Continue to be dependable and keep your promises. Reliability reinforces the trust built over time.

7. **Seek Growth Together**: Engage in activities that promote growth and self-improvement together. Shared experiences and personal growth strengthen the connection and trust.

## Common Challenges to Building Trust

1. **Past Experiences**: Previous negative experiences or betrayals can make it difficult to trust. Recognizing and addressing these past issues is crucial for building trust in new relationships.

2. **Insecurity and Fear**: Insecurities and fear of vulnerability can hinder trust. Building self-confidence and addressing fears can help overcome these challenges.

3. **Communication Issues**: Poor communication can lead to misunderstandings and erode trust. Improving communication skills and fostering open dialogue can address these issues.

4. **External Influences**: External factors, such as stress or negative influences, can impact trust. Managing external stressors and creating a supportive environment can help maintain trust.

5. **Jealousy and Suspicion**: Jealousy and suspicion can undermine trust. Addressing the root causes of these feelings and fostering open communication can mitigate their impact.

## Rebuilding Trust After Betrayal

Rebuilding trust after a betrayal is a challenging but possible process. It requires commitment, patience, and effort from both parties. Here are some steps to rebuild trust:

1. **Acknowledge the Betrayal**: Acknowledge the betrayal and its impact on the relationship. Honest acknowledgment is the first step toward healing.

2. **Offer Sincere Apologies**: Offer sincere apologies for the betrayal. Taking responsibility and expressing genuine remorse is crucial for rebuilding trust.

3. **Open Communication**: Engage in open and honest communication about the betrayal. Discuss the emotions and concerns that arise, and listen empathetically to each other.

4. **Set Clear Boundaries**: Establish clear boundaries and expectations moving forward. Clear boundaries help create a sense of security and prevent future betrayals.

5. **Consistent Actions**: Demonstrate consistent, trustworthy behavior over time. Rebuilding trust requires a sustained commitment to reliability and transparency.

6. **Seek Professional Support**: Consider seeking professional support, such as couples therapy, to navigate the process of rebuilding trust. Professional guidance can provide valuable tools and strategies.

7. **Practice Patience**: Be patient and allow time for healing. Rebuilding trust is a gradual process that requires time and effort from both parties.

**Practical Exercises to Foster Trust**

Here are some practical exercises to help build and maintain trust in relationships:

1. **Trust-Building Activities**: Engage in trust-building activities, such as team-building exercises or problem-solving tasks, to reinforce mutual reliance and collaboration.

2. **Honesty Pacts**: Create honesty pacts where both partners commit to complete transparency and truthfulness in their interactions.

3. **Shared Goals**: Set shared goals and work towards achieving them together. Collaborative efforts strengthen the sense of partnership and trust.

4. **Regular Relationship Check-Ins**: Schedule regular relationship check-ins to discuss the state of the relationship, address concerns, and celebrate successes.

5. **Empathy Exercises**: Practice empathy exercises, such as perspective-taking and active listening, to enhance understanding and trust.

6. **Accountability Partners**: Act as accountability partners for each other, supporting each other's commitments and goals.

7. **Gratitude Journals**: Maintain gratitude journals and regularly share entries with each other. Expressing appreciation for each other's positive actions reinforces trust.

## Conclusion

Trust is the cornerstone of intimacy, providing the foundation for emotional, physical, and psychological closeness. Building and maintaining trust requires consistent honesty, open communication, and mutual respect. By addressing common challenges and practicing trust-building strategies, individuals can create and sustain a trusting environment that enhances intimacy and overall relationship satisfaction.

In the next chapter, we will explore the role of intellectual intimacy in relationships. We will discuss how sharing ideas, engaging in stimulating conversations, and appreciating each other's intellect contribute to a deeper connection. Join us as we continue to delve into the various dimensions of intimacy and their impact on our lives.

# CHAPTER 5: COMMUNICATION: THE KEY TO INTIMACY

Effective communication is crucial for developing and sustaining intimacy. This chapter provides insights into the importance of open and honest communication, offering strategies for improving communication skills and resolving conflicts.

## Understanding the Role of Communication in Intimacy

Communication is the foundation of any relationship. It is through communication that we express our thoughts, feelings, needs, and desires. In the context of intimacy, communication fosters understanding, builds trust, and strengthens emotional connections. It allows individuals to share their innermost thoughts and experiences, creating a deeper bond.

## The Importance of Open and Honest Communication

1. **Building Trust**: Open and honest communication is essential for building trust. When partners communicate transparently, they demonstrate reliability and integrity, fostering a trusting relationship.

2. **Enhancing Emotional Connection**: Sharing

thoughts and feelings openly helps deepen emotional connections. It allows partners to understand each other on a deeper level, creating a sense of closeness and empathy.

3. **Conflict Resolution**: Effective communication is key to resolving conflicts. It enables partners to address issues constructively, express their perspectives, and find mutually acceptable solutions.

4. **Preventing Misunderstandings**: Clear communication helps prevent misunderstandings and misinterpretations. When partners communicate openly, they are less likely to make assumptions and more likely to understand each other accurately.

5. **Fostering Mutual Respect**: Open communication fosters mutual respect by acknowledging and valuing each other's thoughts and feelings. It promotes a balanced and respectful relationship.

## Strategies for Improving Communication Skills

1. **Active Listening**: Active listening involves fully focusing on the speaker, understanding their message, and responding thoughtfully. It requires patience, attention, and empathy. Practice active listening by making eye contact, nodding, and providing verbal affirmations.

2. **Expressing Emotions Clearly**: Clearly expressing emotions involves using "I" statements to communicate feelings without blaming or criticizing. For example, say "I feel hurt when..." instead of "You always make me feel..."

3. **Being Honest and Transparent**: Honesty and transparency are crucial for effective communication. Share your thoughts and feelings

openly, and encourage your partner to do the same.

4. **Avoiding Assumptions**: Avoid making assumptions about your partner's thoughts, feelings, or intentions. Instead, ask clarifying questions to ensure understanding.

5. **Practicing Empathy**: Empathy involves understanding and sharing the feelings of another person. Practice empathy by putting yourself in your partner's shoes and responding with compassion.

6. **Timing and Setting**: Choose the right time and setting for important conversations. Ensure that both partners are in a calm and receptive state, free from distractions.

7. **Non-Verbal Communication**: Pay attention to non-verbal cues, such as body language, facial expressions, and tone of voice. Non-verbal communication can convey emotions and intentions more powerfully than words.

8. **Being Open to Feedback**: Be open to receiving feedback from your partner. Listen to their perspective without becoming defensive, and use the feedback to improve communication.

## Effective Conflict Resolution

Conflicts are a natural part of any relationship. How conflicts are managed can significantly impact intimacy and relationship satisfaction. Here are strategies for effective conflict resolution:

1. **Stay Calm and Composed**: Approach conflicts with a calm and composed demeanor. Avoid reacting impulsively or letting emotions escalate.

2. **Focus on the Issue, Not the Person**: Address the specific issue at hand rather than attacking your partner's character. Use constructive language and

avoid personal attacks.

3. **Use "I" Statements**: Use "I" statements to express your feelings and needs. This approach focuses on your experience rather than blaming your partner.

4. **Listen Actively**: Listen actively to your partner's perspective without interrupting. Validate their feelings and show empathy.

5. **Seek Common Ground**: Identify areas of agreement and common ground. Focus on shared goals and interests to find mutually acceptable solutions.

6. **Take Breaks if Needed**: If emotions become overwhelming, take a break and revisit the conversation when both partners are calmer. Ensure that breaks are used constructively and not as a way to avoid addressing the issue.

7. **Practice Compromise**: Be willing to compromise and find solutions that work for both partners. Compromise involves give-and-take and finding a middle ground.

8. **Seek Professional Help if Needed**: If conflicts persist or become unmanageable, consider seeking professional help, such as couples therapy. Professional support can provide valuable tools and strategies for conflict resolution.

**Practical Exercises to Improve Communication**

Here are some practical exercises to help improve communication skills in relationships:

1. **Active Listening Practice**: Set aside time for active listening practice. Take turns sharing thoughts and feelings while the other partner listens attentively without interrupting.

2. **Daily Check-Ins**: Schedule daily check-ins to discuss

your day, share experiences, and express feelings. Regular check-ins foster open communication and emotional connection.

3. **Communication Journals**: Maintain communication journals where each partner can write down their thoughts and feelings. Share journal entries with each other to facilitate understanding and empathy.

4. **Role-Playing**: Engage in role-playing exercises to practice difficult conversations. Role-playing helps build communication skills and prepares partners for real-life interactions.

5. **Feedback Sessions**: Schedule regular feedback sessions where each partner can share constructive feedback. Use these sessions to discuss areas for improvement and celebrate successes.

6. **Mindful Communication**: Practice mindful communication by being fully present during conversations. Focus on the present moment and avoid distractions.

7. **Expressing Appreciation**: Regularly express appreciation for your partner's positive actions and qualities. Acknowledging each other's efforts fosters a positive communication environment.

**Overcoming Communication Barriers**

Several barriers can hinder effective communication. Recognizing and addressing these barriers is crucial for fostering intimacy:

1. **Fear of Vulnerability**: Fear of vulnerability can prevent open communication. Building trust and creating a safe space for sharing can help overcome this fear.

2. **Cultural Differences**: Cultural differences can impact communication styles and expectations.

Respecting and understanding each other's cultural backgrounds can enhance communication.

3. **Past Experiences**: Past negative experiences or traumas can affect communication. Seeking professional support and engaging in healing practices can address these issues.

4. **Stress and Fatigue**: Stress and fatigue can impair communication. Managing stress through relaxation techniques and ensuring adequate rest can improve communication.

5. **Technology Distractions**: Technology can be a distraction during conversations. Create technology-free zones or times to focus on face-to-face communication.

## Conclusion

Effective communication is the key to intimacy, fostering understanding, trust, and emotional connection. By practicing active listening, expressing emotions clearly, and addressing conflicts constructively, individuals can enhance their communication skills and deepen their relationships.

In the next chapter, we will explore the concept of intellectual intimacy. We will discuss how sharing ideas, engaging in stimulating conversations, and appreciating each other's intellect contribute to a deeper connection. Join us as we continue to delve into the various dimensions of intimacy and their impact on our lives.

# CHAPTER 6: INTIMACY IN FRIENDSHIPS

Intimacy is not limited to romantic relationships; it is also a vital component of close friendships. This chapter discusses the unique aspects of intimacy in friendships, highlighting the importance of emotional support and shared experiences.

**The Nature of Intimate Friendships**

Friendships are a fundamental part of our social lives, providing companionship, support, and a sense of belonging. Intimate friendships go beyond casual acquaintances and involve a deeper level of emotional connection and mutual understanding. These friendships are characterized by trust, loyalty, and a shared sense of identity and values.

**Emotional Support in Friendships**

1. **Understanding and Empathy**: Intimate friends offer a high degree of understanding and empathy. They listen without judgment and provide a safe space for expressing feelings and concerns.

2. **Reliability and Dependability**: Reliable friends are there during times of need, offering support and assistance. This dependability fosters a sense of security and trust.

3. **Validation and Affirmation**: Intimate friends validate each other's experiences and feelings. They

offer affirmation, boosting each other's self-esteem and confidence.

4. **Emotional Availability**: Being emotionally available means being present and attentive to a friend's needs. This availability strengthens the emotional bond and fosters intimacy.

5. **Non-Judgmental Support**: True friends offer support without criticism or judgment. This non-judgmental approach encourages open and honest communication.

## Shared Experiences in Friendships

1. **Common Interests and Activities**: Shared interests and activities form the basis of many intimate friendships. Engaging in common hobbies and pastimes creates lasting memories and strengthens bonds.

2. **Celebrating Milestones**: Celebrating life milestones together, such as birthdays, graduations, and achievements, enhances the sense of shared experience and connection.

3. **Overcoming Challenges Together**: Facing and overcoming challenges together, whether personal or external, deepens the bond and builds resilience within the friendship.

4. **Travel and Adventure**: Traveling and embarking on adventures together create unique and memorable experiences. These shared experiences foster a sense of camaraderie and closeness.

5. **Everyday Moments**: Simple, everyday moments, such as conversations over coffee or movie nights, contribute to the intimacy of friendships. These moments build a strong foundation of familiarity and comfort.

## Building Intimacy in Friendships

1. **Open Communication**: Foster open and honest communication. Share thoughts, feelings, and experiences openly, and encourage your friends to do the same.

2. **Active Listening**: Practice active listening by giving your full attention, making eye contact, and responding thoughtfully. Show genuine interest in your friend's experiences and emotions.

3. **Being Present**: Be present and attentive in your interactions. Avoid distractions and focus on the moment to show that you value your friend's company.

4. **Expressing Appreciation**: Regularly express appreciation for your friend's presence and support. Acknowledge their positive qualities and the value they bring to your life.

5. **Offering Support**: Be there for your friends during times of need. Offer emotional, practical, and moral support, demonstrating your reliability and care.

6. **Respecting Boundaries**: Respect your friend's boundaries and personal space. Acknowledge their needs and preferences, and avoid pushing them beyond their comfort zone.

7. **Sharing Vulnerabilities**: Share your vulnerabilities and encourage your friends to do the same. Vulnerability fosters a deeper emotional connection and mutual trust.

8. **Quality Time**: Spend quality time together. Engage in activities that you both enjoy and that strengthen your bond.

## Maintaining Intimacy in Friendships

1. **Consistent Communication**: Maintain regular communication, whether through in-person meetings, phone calls, or messages. Consistent communication keeps the connection strong.

2. **Handling Conflicts Gracefully**: Address conflicts with empathy and understanding. Use effective communication and conflict resolution skills to navigate disagreements constructively.

3. **Adapting to Changes**: Friendships may evolve over time due to life changes, such as moving, changing jobs, or starting families. Adapt to these changes by finding new ways to stay connected.

4. **Mutual Support**: Offer mutual support by being both a giver and a receiver. Balance the dynamic of support to ensure that both friends feel valued and cared for.

5. **Celebrating Differences**: Embrace and celebrate each other's differences. Diversity in perspectives and experiences can enrich the friendship and foster mutual respect.

6. **Practicing Forgiveness**: Practice forgiveness when misunderstandings or mistakes occur. Holding onto grudges can damage the friendship, while forgiveness promotes healing and growth.

## The Unique Aspects of Intimate Friendships

1. **Non-Romantic Love**: Intimate friendships involve a deep sense of love and affection that is non-romantic. This platonic love is characterized by care, loyalty, and emotional closeness.

2. **Lifelong Connections**: Many intimate friendships are lifelong connections that withstand the test of time. These enduring relationships provide stability and a sense of continuity.

3. **Freedom from Expectations**: Unlike romantic relationships, intimate friendships often come with fewer societal expectations and pressures. This freedom allows for a more relaxed and genuine connection.

4. **Emotional Resilience**: Intimate friendships contribute to emotional resilience. Having a strong support system of friends can help individuals navigate life's challenges more effectively.

5. **Shared Identity and Values**: Intimate friends often share similar values, beliefs, and interests. This shared identity strengthens the bond and fosters a sense of belonging.

**Practical Exercises to Foster Intimacy in Friendships**

1. **Regular Check-Ins**: Schedule regular check-ins to discuss your lives, share experiences, and provide support. Consistent communication strengthens the emotional connection.

2. **Joint Activities**: Engage in joint activities that you both enjoy, such as hobbies, sports, or creative projects. Shared activities create lasting memories and enhance the bond.

3. **Empathy Exercises**: Practice empathy exercises, such as perspective-taking and active listening, to enhance understanding and emotional connection.

4. **Gratitude Journals**: Maintain gratitude journals and share entries with each other. Expressing appreciation for your friend's positive actions reinforces intimacy.

5. **Trust-Building Activities**: Participate in trust-building activities, such as team-building exercises or problem-solving tasks, to reinforce mutual reliance and collaboration.

6. **Supportive Challenges**: Set and pursue personal or shared goals together. Support each other in achieving these goals, fostering a sense of partnership and mutual encouragement.

7. **Reflective Conversations**: Have reflective conversations about your friendship. Discuss what you value in the relationship and how you can continue to support each other.

## Conclusion

Intimacy in friendships is a vital component of our social lives, providing emotional support, shared experiences, and a sense of belonging. By fostering open communication, offering support, and engaging in shared activities, individuals can build and maintain intimate friendships that enhance their overall well-being.

In the next chapter, we will explore the role of intellectual intimacy in relationships. We will discuss how sharing ideas, engaging in stimulating conversations, and appreciating each other's intellect contribute to a deeper connection. Join us as we continue to delve into the various dimensions of intimacy and their impact on our lives.

# CHAPTER 7: ROMANTIC INTIMACY: A DEEP DIVE

Romantic intimacy involves a combination of emotional, physical, and sexual closeness. This chapter explores the complexities of romantic intimacy, offering advice on how to cultivate and maintain a deep, loving connection with a partner.

**Understanding Romantic Intimacy**

Romantic intimacy is a multifaceted and dynamic aspect of relationships that combines emotional, physical, and sexual closeness. It involves a deep connection that fosters love, trust, and mutual respect. Romantic intimacy is characterized by the following elements:

1. **Emotional Closeness**: Sharing thoughts, feelings, and experiences, and providing emotional support and understanding.

2. **Physical Closeness**: Engaging in non-sexual physical touch, such as hugging, holding hands, and cuddling, which strengthens the bond.

3. **Sexual Closeness**: Engaging in sexual activities that are mutually satisfying and enhance the connection between partners.

**The Importance of Emotional Intimacy in Romantic Relationships**

Emotional intimacy is the foundation of a strong romantic relationship. It involves being open and vulnerable with your partner, sharing your innermost thoughts and feelings, and providing and receiving emotional support. Here are key aspects of emotional intimacy:

1. **Trust**: Trust is the bedrock of emotional intimacy. It involves being reliable, keeping promises, and maintaining confidentiality.

2. **Empathy**: Empathy involves understanding and sharing your partner's emotions. It requires active listening and showing genuine concern for their well-being.

3. **Honesty**: Being honest and transparent with your partner fosters trust and deepens emotional connections.

4. **Vulnerability**: Sharing your vulnerabilities with your partner creates a deeper emotional bond and fosters mutual trust and understanding.

5. **Emotional Support**: Providing emotional support during times of stress, sadness, or joy strengthens the emotional connection.

## Cultivating Physical Intimacy

Physical intimacy is an essential component of romantic relationships. It involves non-sexual physical touch that expresses love, affection, and comfort. Here are ways to cultivate physical intimacy:

1. **Affectionate Touch**: Engage in affectionate touch, such as hugging, holding hands, and cuddling. These actions convey love and strengthen the bond.

2. **Physical Presence**: Spend quality time together, being physically present and attentive to each other.

3. **Comfort and Security**: Use physical touch to provide

comfort and a sense of security, especially during stressful times.

4. **Playfulness**: Engage in playful physical activities, such as dancing, play wrestling, or tickling, to enhance physical intimacy.

## Enhancing Sexual Intimacy

Sexual intimacy is a vital aspect of romantic relationships that involves mutual pleasure and satisfaction. Here are strategies to enhance sexual intimacy:

1. **Communication**: Openly discuss sexual desires, boundaries, and preferences with your partner. Clear communication enhances sexual satisfaction.

2. **Experimentation**: Be open to exploring new activities and experiences that can enhance sexual intimacy.

3. **Focus on Connection**: Prioritize emotional and physical connection over performance. Focus on the pleasure and closeness that sex brings.

4. **Mutual Respect**: Respect each other's boundaries and preferences. Ensure that sexual activities are consensual and mutually enjoyable.

5. **Quality Time**: Set aside time for intimate moments, ensuring that both partners feel valued and desired.

## Building and Maintaining Romantic Intimacy

Building and maintaining romantic intimacy requires effort, commitment, and mutual respect. Here are practical tips to cultivate and sustain intimacy in a romantic relationship:

1. **Prioritize Quality Time**: Spend quality time together, engaging in activities that you both enjoy. Regularly schedule date nights or special moments to connect.

2. **Express Appreciation**: Regularly express

appreciation and gratitude for your partner. Acknowledge their positive qualities and efforts.

3. **Practice Active Listening**: Listen actively to your partner's thoughts and feelings. Show empathy and understanding in your interactions.

4. **Share Goals and Dreams**: Discuss your individual and shared goals and dreams. Supporting each other's aspirations strengthens the bond.

5. **Resolve Conflicts Constructively**: Address conflicts with empathy and understanding. Use effective communication and conflict resolution skills to navigate disagreements.

6. **Maintain Physical Affection**: Keep physical affection alive through regular touch, cuddling, and other forms of non-sexual physical intimacy.

7. **Nurture Emotional Connection**: Continuously nurture your emotional connection by sharing your thoughts, feelings, and experiences.

8. **Be Flexible and Adaptable**: Be flexible and adaptable to changes in the relationship. Life circumstances may evolve, and being open to change helps maintain intimacy.

9. **Support Each Other**: Offer support during times of stress, illness, or challenges. Being there for each other strengthens the bond.

10. **Seek Professional Help if Needed**: If intimacy issues persist, consider seeking professional help, such as couples therapy, to address and resolve underlying issues.

**Practical Exercises to Enhance Romantic Intimacy**

1. **Daily Check-Ins**: Schedule daily check-ins to discuss your day, share experiences, and express feelings.

Regular check-ins foster open communication and emotional connection.

2. **Date Nights**: Plan regular date nights to spend quality time together. Engage in activities that you both enjoy and that strengthen your bond.

3. **Love Letters**: Write love letters to each other, expressing your feelings and appreciation. This practice deepens emotional intimacy.

4. **Shared Hobbies**: Engage in shared hobbies or activities that you both enjoy. Shared experiences create lasting memories and enhance connection.

5. **Mindfulness Exercises**: Practice mindfulness exercises together, such as meditation or deep breathing. Mindfulness enhances emotional and physical connection.

6. **Intimate Conversations**: Have intimate conversations where you discuss your hopes, dreams, and fears. Sharing vulnerabilities fosters emotional intimacy.

7. **Physical Touch Rituals**: Establish physical touch rituals, such as morning hugs or bedtime cuddles, to maintain physical intimacy.

8. **Gratitude Journals**: Maintain gratitude journals and share entries with each other. Expressing appreciation for your partner reinforces intimacy.

## Overcoming Challenges in Romantic Intimacy

Romantic intimacy can face challenges that require attention and effort to overcome. Here are common challenges and strategies to address them:

1. **Communication Barriers**: Address communication barriers by practicing active listening, being honest, and expressing feelings openly.

2. **Stress and Fatigue**: Manage stress and fatigue through relaxation techniques, self-care, and ensuring adequate rest. Prioritize time for intimacy despite busy schedules.

3. **Routine and Monotony**: Combat routine and monotony by introducing new activities, experiences, and surprises into the relationship.

4. **Insecurity and Jealousy**: Address insecurity and jealousy through open communication, building trust, and seeking professional help if needed.

5. **Life Transitions**: Adapt to life transitions, such as moving, job changes, or starting a family, by being flexible and supportive of each other.

**Conclusion**

Romantic intimacy is a dynamic and multifaceted aspect of relationships that involves emotional, physical, and sexual closeness. By prioritizing open communication, emotional support, physical affection, and mutual respect, couples can cultivate and maintain a deep, loving connection.

In the next chapter, we will explore the role of intellectual intimacy in relationships. We will discuss how sharing ideas, engaging in stimulating conversations, and appreciating each other's intellect contribute to a deeper connection. Join us as we continue to delve into the various dimensions of intimacy and their impact on our lives.

# CHAPTER 8: INTIMACY IN MARRIAGE

Marriage is often considered the ultimate expression of romantic intimacy. This chapter examines the dynamics of intimacy within marriage, addressing common challenges and providing practical tips for nurturing a strong, intimate bond.

## Understanding Intimacy in Marriage

Marriage involves a lifelong commitment to a partner, and intimacy plays a crucial role in maintaining a healthy and fulfilling relationship. Intimacy in marriage encompasses emotional, physical, and sexual closeness, and it evolves over time as couples navigate different life stages and challenges. A strong marital bond requires continuous effort and mutual respect, as well as a willingness to grow together.

## Emotional Intimacy in Marriage

1. **Mutual Trust and Respect**: Trust and respect are fundamental to emotional intimacy. Trust is built through reliability, honesty, and consistency, while respect involves valuing each other's opinions, boundaries, and individuality.

2. **Open Communication**: Effective communication is essential for emotional intimacy. Couples should strive to share their thoughts, feelings, and

experiences openly, and listen actively to each other.

3. **Empathy and Understanding**: Empathy involves understanding and sharing your partner's emotions. Demonstrating empathy helps create a supportive and compassionate environment.

4. **Vulnerability**: Being vulnerable means sharing your innermost thoughts and fears with your partner. Vulnerability fosters a deeper emotional connection and trust.

5. **Emotional Support**: Providing emotional support during times of joy and hardship strengthens the bond. Being present and attentive to your partner's needs is crucial.

**Physical Intimacy in Marriage**

1. **Affectionate Touch**: Regular affectionate touch, such as hugging, holding hands, and cuddling, is important for maintaining physical intimacy. These actions express love and reassurance.

2. **Quality Time Together**: Spending quality time together, free from distractions, enhances physical and emotional closeness. Engage in activities that you both enjoy.

3. **Comfort and Security**: Physical touch can provide comfort and a sense of security, especially during stressful times. Simple gestures like a reassuring touch can make a significant difference.

4. **Playfulness**: Incorporate playfulness into your physical interactions. Playful touch and activities help keep the relationship fun and engaging.

5. **Intimacy Rituals**: Establish rituals, such as goodnight kisses or morning hugs, to maintain regular physical connection.

## Sexual Intimacy in Marriage

1. **Communication About Desires**: Openly discussing sexual desires, boundaries, and preferences is essential for a fulfilling sexual relationship. Clear communication enhances mutual satisfaction.

2. **Exploration and Experimentation**: Be open to exploring new activities and experiences in your sexual relationship. Experimentation can keep the sexual connection exciting and fulfilling.

3. **Mutual Consent and Respect**: Always respect each other's boundaries and ensure that all sexual activities are consensual. Mutual respect is key to a healthy sexual relationship.

4. **Emotional Connection**: Prioritize the emotional connection in your sexual relationship. Emotional intimacy often enhances sexual intimacy, making the experience more meaningful.

5. **Regular Intimacy**: Maintain a regular sexual connection that works for both partners. Regular intimacy helps keep the bond strong and ensures that both partners feel desired and valued.

## Common Challenges in Marital Intimacy

1. **Communication Breakdowns**: Miscommunication or lack of communication can lead to misunderstandings and distance. Regularly check in with each other and strive for open, honest dialogue.

2. **Stress and Fatigue**: Daily stressors and fatigue can affect intimacy. Find ways to manage stress together and prioritize rest and relaxation.

3. **Routine and Monotony**: Routine and predictability can lead to a lack of excitement. Introduce new activities, experiences, and spontaneity to keep the relationship dynamic.

4. **Life Transitions**: Major life changes, such as having children, career changes, or moving, can impact intimacy. Adapt to these changes by being supportive and flexible.

5. **Conflict and Resentment**: Unresolved conflicts and built-up resentment can erode intimacy. Address conflicts constructively and practice forgiveness to heal and move forward.

**Practical Tips for Nurturing Intimacy in Marriage**

1. **Prioritize Your Relationship**: Make your relationship a priority amidst other responsibilities. Regularly set aside time for each other.

2. **Express Appreciation**: Regularly express appreciation for your partner's qualities, efforts, and contributions. Acknowledge the positive aspects of your relationship.

3. **Practice Active Listening**: Listen actively and attentively to your partner. Show empathy and validate their feelings and experiences.

4. **Engage in Shared Activities**: Participate in activities that you both enjoy. Shared experiences create lasting memories and strengthen the bond.

5. **Keep the Romance Alive**: Continue to court each other and keep the romance alive. Plan date nights, surprise each other, and express your love in creative ways.

6. **Work on Self-Improvement**: Personal growth and self-improvement contribute to a healthier relationship. Encourage and support each other's individual growth.

7. **Seek Professional Help if Needed**: If intimacy issues persist, consider seeking professional help, such as couples therapy. Professional guidance can provide

new perspectives and solutions.

**Practical Exercises to Enhance Intimacy in Marriage**

1. **Daily Check-Ins**: Schedule daily check-ins to discuss your day, share experiences, and express feelings. Regular check-ins foster open communication and emotional connection.

2. **Date Nights**: Plan regular date nights to spend quality time together. Engage in activities that you both enjoy and that strengthen your bond.

3. **Love Letters**: Write love letters to each other, expressing your feelings and appreciation. This practice deepens emotional intimacy.

4. **Shared Hobbies**: Engage in shared hobbies or activities that you both enjoy. Shared experiences create lasting memories and enhance connection.

5. **Mindfulness Exercises**: Practice mindfulness exercises together, such as meditation or deep breathing. Mindfulness enhances emotional and physical connection.

6. **Intimate Conversations**: Have intimate conversations where you discuss your hopes, dreams, and fears. Sharing vulnerabilities fosters emotional intimacy.

7. **Physical Touch Rituals**: Establish physical touch rituals, such as morning hugs or bedtime cuddles, to maintain physical intimacy.

8. **Gratitude Journals**: Maintain gratitude journals and share entries with each other. Expressing appreciation for your partner reinforces intimacy.

**Conclusion**

Intimacy in marriage is a multifaceted and evolving aspect of the relationship that requires continuous effort and mutual respect. By prioritizing open communication, emotional support, physical affection, and mutual respect, couples can cultivate and maintain a deep, loving connection that withstands the test of time.

In the next chapter, we will explore the role of intellectual intimacy in relationships. We will discuss how sharing ideas, engaging in stimulating conversations, and appreciating each other's intellect contribute to a deeper connection. Join us as we continue to delve into the various dimensions of intimacy and their impact on our lives.

# CHAPTER 9: INTIMACY AND VULNERABILITY

Vulnerability is an integral part of intimacy, allowing individuals to share their true selves without fear of judgment. This chapter explores the role of vulnerability in fostering deep connections and offers guidance on how to embrace vulnerability in relationships.

**Understanding Vulnerability in Relationships**

Vulnerability involves exposing one's true self, including fears, insecurities, and emotional needs. It requires courage and trust, as it involves revealing aspects of oneself that are often kept hidden. Vulnerability is essential for creating deep, authentic connections in relationships, as it fosters trust, empathy, and mutual understanding.

**The Role of Vulnerability in Intimacy**

1. **Fostering Trust**: When individuals are vulnerable, they demonstrate trust in their partner. This openness can lead to a deeper level of mutual trust and a stronger emotional bond.

2. **Enhancing Emotional Connection**: Sharing vulnerabilities allows partners to understand each other on a deeper level. This emotional connection fosters a sense of closeness and intimacy.

3. **Building Empathy**: Vulnerability encourages

empathy by allowing partners to see each other's struggles and emotions. This understanding creates a supportive and compassionate environment.

4. **Encouraging Authenticity**: Being vulnerable allows individuals to present their true selves. Authenticity strengthens relationships by promoting honesty and openness.

5. **Reducing Fear of Judgment**: When vulnerability is met with acceptance and support, it reduces the fear of judgment. This acceptance promotes a safe space for honest communication.

## The Benefits of Embracing Vulnerability

1. **Deepening Connections**: Vulnerability fosters deeper emotional connections, as it allows individuals to connect on a more personal level.

2. **Promoting Emotional Growth**: Embracing vulnerability can lead to personal growth and emotional resilience. It encourages individuals to confront and address their fears and insecurities.

3. **Strengthening Relationships**: Vulnerability strengthens relationships by building trust and enhancing emotional intimacy. It creates a foundation of mutual respect and understanding.

4. **Enhancing Communication**: Openly sharing vulnerabilities improves communication by fostering honesty and reducing misunderstandings.

5. **Increasing Intimacy**: Vulnerability is a key component of intimacy, as it allows individuals to share their innermost thoughts and feelings, leading to a more profound connection.

## Overcoming Barriers to Vulnerability

1. **Fear of Rejection**: Fear of rejection can hinder

vulnerability. To overcome this fear, focus on building a supportive and accepting environment within the relationship.

2. **Past Trauma**: Past experiences of betrayal or hurt can make vulnerability challenging. Addressing past trauma with professional support can help individuals become more comfortable with vulnerability.

3. **Perceived Weakness**: Some individuals perceive vulnerability as a sign of weakness. Reframe vulnerability as a strength and a courageous act of openness.

4. **Trust Issues**: Trust issues can impact one's ability to be vulnerable. Building and maintaining trust through consistent actions and honest communication is crucial.

5. **Cultural and Social Norms**: Cultural and social norms can influence attitudes toward vulnerability. Challenge and redefine these norms within the context of your relationship.

**Strategies for Embracing Vulnerability**

1. **Start Small**: Begin by sharing small, manageable aspects of your thoughts and feelings. Gradually increase the level of vulnerability as you build confidence.

2. **Be Honest and Open**: Practice honesty and openness in your interactions. Share your true feelings, thoughts, and experiences with your partner.

3. **Communicate Clearly**: Clearly communicate your needs and emotions. Use "I" statements to express how you feel and what you need from your partner.

4. **Create a Safe Space**: Foster a safe and supportive environment for vulnerability. Show acceptance

and understanding in response to your partner's openness.

5. **Encourage Mutual Vulnerability**: Encourage your partner to share their vulnerabilities as well. Mutual vulnerability strengthens the emotional connection and builds trust.

6. **Practice Self-Compassion**: Be kind to yourself when you experience discomfort or fear related to vulnerability. Self-compassion can help you navigate the challenges of being open.

7. **Seek Support**: If vulnerability is particularly challenging, seek support from a therapist or counselor. Professional guidance can provide strategies and tools for embracing vulnerability.

**Practical Exercises to Foster Vulnerability**

1. **Vulnerability Journals**: Keep a journal where you explore and write about your fears, insecurities, and emotional needs. Share relevant entries with your partner to facilitate open conversations.

2. **Vulnerability Conversations**: Schedule regular conversations with your partner to discuss your feelings, experiences, and fears. Create a safe space for these discussions.

3. **Gratitude Sharing**: Share what you appreciate about each other and express gratitude for each other's support and acceptance. This practice fosters a positive and accepting environment.

4. **Affectionate Gestures**: Use affectionate gestures to express your vulnerability and appreciation. Simple acts of kindness, such as hugs or notes of encouragement, can strengthen the bond.

5. **Emotional Check-Ins**: Regularly check in with each other about your emotional well-being. Share how

you are feeling and listen actively to your partner's emotions.

6. **Role Reversal Exercises**: Engage in role reversal exercises where you take on each other's perspectives. This practice can increase empathy and understanding.

7. **Vulnerability Challenges**: Set small challenges for yourself to practice vulnerability. For example, share a personal story or express a concern that you have been keeping to yourself.

**Addressing Common Misconceptions About Vulnerability**

1. **Misconception: Vulnerability Equals Weakness**: Vulnerability is often perceived as a sign of weakness, but it is actually a sign of strength and courage. It requires bravery to expose one's true self.

2. **Misconception: Vulnerability Leads to Rejection**: While vulnerability does carry the risk of rejection, it also opens the door to deeper connections and understanding. Rejection can be a part of the process, but it is not the end result.

3. **Misconception: Vulnerability Is Only for Romantic Relationships**: Vulnerability is important in all types of relationships, including friendships and family connections. It fosters deeper bonds and mutual understanding in various contexts.

4. **Misconception: Vulnerability Can Be Controlled**: Vulnerability is a natural and unpredictable aspect of relationships. It cannot be entirely controlled, but it can be embraced and nurtured.

5. **Misconception: Vulnerability Means Sharing Everything**: Vulnerability involves sharing what feels appropriate and relevant to the relationship. It does not mean sharing every detail of one's life, but

rather being open about what matters most.

## Conclusion

Vulnerability is a powerful and essential component of intimacy. It allows individuals to share their true selves, fostering trust, empathy, and deep emotional connections. Embracing vulnerability requires courage and a supportive environment, but the rewards are profound. By practicing openness, honesty, and self-compassion, individuals can enhance their relationships and create deeper, more meaningful connections.

In the next chapter, we will explore the role of intellectual intimacy in relationships. We will discuss how sharing ideas, engaging in stimulating conversations, and appreciating each other's intellect contribute to a deeper connection. Join us as we continue to delve into the various dimensions of intimacy and their impact on our lives.

# CHAPTER 10: OVERCOMING BARRIERS TO INTIMACY

Intimacy is crucial for forming deep, meaningful connections, but various factors can hinder its development. Barriers to intimacy may stem from past traumas, communication issues, personal insecurities, and other challenges. This chapter identifies common barriers to intimacy and provides strategies for overcoming them.

**Identifying Common Barriers to Intimacy**

1. **Past Traumas**: Experiences of betrayal, abuse, or other forms of trauma can create significant barriers to intimacy. These past wounds may lead to trust issues, emotional distance, and difficulty in forming close connections.

2. **Communication Issues**: Ineffective communication can hinder intimacy by creating misunderstandings, conflicts, and emotional distance. Poor communication skills, such as lack of active listening or expressing emotions, can impede connection.

3. **Personal Insecurities**: Insecurities about oneself, such as feelings of inadequacy, low self-esteem, or body image issues, can affect one's ability to be open

and vulnerable in relationships.

4. **Fear of Rejection**: The fear of being rejected or judged can prevent individuals from expressing their true selves and sharing their emotions. This fear can create emotional barriers and hinder intimacy.

5. **Cultural and Social Norms**: Cultural and social expectations can influence attitudes toward intimacy and vulnerability. These norms may discourage openness or prioritize emotional restraint.

6. **Stress and Fatigue**: High levels of stress or fatigue can impact emotional availability and reduce the capacity for intimacy. Life demands and exhaustion can create emotional barriers.

7. **Unresolved Conflicts**: Lingering conflicts or unresolved issues can create emotional distance and hinder intimacy. Unaddressed grievances can lead to resentment and a breakdown in connection.

8. **Different Relationship Goals**: Misalignment in relationship goals and expectations can create friction and hinder intimacy. Differences in values, priorities, or future plans can affect the depth of connection.

**Strategies for Overcoming Barriers to Intimacy**

1. **Addressing Past Traumas**
   - **Seek Professional Help**: Engage with a therapist or counselor to work through past traumas and their impact on current relationships. Professional support can provide tools for healing and rebuilding trust.

   - **Practice Self-Compassion**: Develop self-compassion by recognizing and accepting past wounds. Treat yourself with kindness and understanding as you work through these issues.

- **Communicate with Partners**: Share relevant aspects of past traumas with your partner, if comfortable. This openness can foster understanding and support within the relationship.

2. **Improving Communication Skills**
   - **Practice Active Listening**: Focus on listening attentively to your partner's thoughts and feelings. Reflect on what you hear and validate their emotions.

   - **Use "I" Statements**: Communicate your feelings and needs using "I" statements to express yourself without placing blame. For example, say, "I feel upset when..." rather than "You always..."

   - **Seek Feedback**: Request feedback from your partner on your communication style and work on areas that may need improvement.

3. **Building Self-Esteem and Addressing Insecurities**
   - **Engage in Self-Reflection**: Identify and challenge negative self-beliefs. Practice positive self-talk and affirmations to build self-esteem.

   - **Focus on Strengths**: Recognize and celebrate your strengths and accomplishments. Developing self-confidence helps improve your ability to be open and vulnerable.

   - **Work on Self-Care**: Engage in activities that promote well-being and self-care. Taking care of yourself physically, emotionally, and mentally can enhance self-esteem.

4. **Managing Fear of Rejection**
   - **Reframe Rejection**: View rejection as a natural part of relationships and personal growth. Understand that rejection does not define your worth or ability to connect.
   - **Build Resilience**: Develop emotional resilience by practicing self-compassion and learning from experiences. Resilience helps you cope with rejection and continue to seek meaningful connections.
   - **Communicate Openly**: Share your fears and concerns with your partner. Open communication can alleviate anxiety and foster a supportive environment.

5. **Challenging Cultural and Social Norms**
   - **Explore Personal Beliefs**: Reflect on cultural and social norms that influence your attitudes toward intimacy. Challenge and redefine these beliefs within the context of your relationship.
   - **Encourage Open Dialogue**: Promote open discussions about cultural expectations and their impact on your relationship. Understanding each other's perspectives fosters mutual respect.
   - **Seek Diverse Perspectives**: Engage with diverse viewpoints on intimacy and vulnerability. Exposure to different perspectives can broaden your understanding and acceptance.

6. **Managing Stress and Fatigue**

- **Prioritize Self-Care**: Incorporate self-care practices into your routine to manage stress and fatigue. Activities such as exercise, relaxation techniques, and hobbies can improve emotional well-being.

- **Set Boundaries**: Establish boundaries to manage work and personal demands. Ensure that you have time for relaxation and quality time with your partner.

- **Practice Stress-Relief Techniques**: Utilize stress-relief techniques such as meditation, deep breathing, or mindfulness to reduce stress levels and enhance emotional availability.

7. **Resolving Unresolved Conflicts**

- **Address Issues Promptly**: Tackle conflicts and disagreements as they arise. Avoid letting issues fester by addressing them in a timely and constructive manner.

- **Practice Constructive Conflict Resolution**: Use conflict resolution techniques, such as active listening, empathy, and compromise, to resolve disputes and strengthen the relationship.

- **Seek Mediation if Needed**: If conflicts persist, consider seeking mediation or professional help to address and resolve ongoing issues.

8. **Aligning Relationship Goals**

- **Discuss Expectations**: Have open discussions about relationship goals, values, and expectations. Ensure that both partners are on the same page regarding future plans and priorities.

- ◦ **Negotiate Compromises**: Work together to find common ground and negotiate compromises when differences arise. Flexibility and willingness to adapt can help align goals.

- ◦ **Revisit Goals Regularly**: Periodically revisit and discuss relationship goals to ensure that they remain aligned. Adjustments may be necessary as circumstances change.

**Practical Exercises to Overcome Barriers**

1. **Journaling**: Use journaling to explore and reflect on barriers to intimacy. Write about past traumas, insecurities, and communication issues to gain insights and identify patterns.

2. **Role-Playing**: Engage in role-playing exercises to practice communication skills and address conflicts. Role-playing can help improve understanding and empathy.

3. **Self-Esteem Building Activities**: Participate in activities that promote self-esteem and confidence, such as setting and achieving personal goals or engaging in positive affirmations.

4. **Stress Management Techniques**: Practice stress management techniques, such as mindfulness or relaxation exercises, to reduce stress and improve emotional availability.

5. **Conflict Resolution Workshops**: Attend workshops or seminars on conflict resolution and communication skills to enhance your ability to address and resolve issues.

6. **Goal Setting Exercises**: Set and discuss relationship goals with your partner. Use goal-setting exercises to ensure alignment and work towards shared

objectives.

## Conclusion

Overcoming barriers to intimacy requires effort, self-awareness, and effective strategies. By addressing past traumas, improving communication skills, building self-esteem, managing fear of rejection, challenging cultural norms, and resolving conflicts, individuals can enhance their capacity for deep, meaningful connections. Embracing these strategies fosters a supportive and understanding environment, allowing intimacy to flourish.

In the next chapter, we will explore the role of intellectual intimacy in relationships. We will discuss how sharing ideas, engaging in stimulating conversations, and appreciating each other's intellect contribute to a deeper connection. Join us as we continue to delve into the various dimensions of intimacy and their impact on our lives.

# CHAPTER 11: THE ROLE OF EMPATHY

Empathy is the ability to understand and share the feelings of another person. It involves putting yourself in someone else's shoes and experiencing their emotions and perspectives. This chapter discusses the importance of empathy in building intimate connections and offers practical tips for developing empathetic skills.

**Understanding Empathy**

Empathy is more than just feeling sympathy for someone; it involves deeply understanding their emotions and experiences. Empathy allows individuals to connect on an emotional level, fostering stronger relationships and enhancing mutual understanding.

1. **Cognitive Empathy**: This refers to the ability to understand another person's thoughts and perspective. It involves recognizing and comprehending how others perceive situations and events.

2. **Emotional Empathy**: This involves sharing or mirroring another person's emotions. It means feeling what someone else is feeling, which helps in building emotional connections.

3. **Compassionate Empathy**: This goes beyond understanding and sharing feelings to include a desire to help or support the other person. It combines cognitive and emotional empathy with

actionable compassion.

## The Importance of Empathy in Building Intimate Connections

1. **Fostering Understanding**: Empathy helps individuals understand each other's feelings, thoughts, and experiences. This understanding creates a foundation for deeper emotional connections.

2. **Enhancing Communication**: Empathetic listening and responses improve communication by validating and acknowledging the other person's feelings. This leads to more effective and meaningful conversations.

3. **Building Trust**: When individuals show empathy, they demonstrate that they care about the other person's well-being. This builds trust and strengthens the bond in the relationship.

4. **Resolving Conflicts**: Empathy allows individuals to see conflicts from multiple perspectives, facilitating conflict resolution. Understanding each other's viewpoints helps in finding common ground and solutions.

5. **Promoting Emotional Support**: Empathy enables individuals to offer appropriate emotional support and comfort. By understanding and sharing feelings, individuals can provide meaningful and supportive responses.

6. **Encouraging Emotional Growth**: Empathy encourages personal and emotional growth by exposing individuals to different perspectives and experiences. It helps individuals develop a broader understanding of human emotions.

## Developing Empathetic Skills

1. **Active Listening**: Practice active listening by fully focusing on the speaker, avoiding interruptions, and reflecting on what they are saying. This demonstrates attentiveness and validates their feelings.
    - **Techniques for Active Listening**:
        - **Reflective Listening**: Paraphrase or summarize what the other person has said to show understanding.
        - **Open-Ended Questions**: Ask questions that encourage the other person to elaborate on their feelings and experiences.
        - **Nonverbal Cues**: Use nonverbal cues such as nodding and maintaining eye contact to show engagement and understanding.

2. **Ask Questions and Seek Clarification**: To deepen your understanding, ask questions that invite the other person to share more about their feelings and perspective. Seeking clarification helps ensure accurate comprehension.

3. **Practice Perspective-Taking**: Make a conscious effort to imagine yourself in the other person's situation. Consider how you would feel and react if you were in their position.

4. **Validate Feelings**: Acknowledge and validate the other person's emotions, even if you do not fully understand or agree with their perspective. Validation shows that you respect their feelings and experiences.

5. **Be Present**: Focus on being fully present in interactions. Avoid distractions and give your complete attention to the person you are

communicating with.

6. **Share Your Own Feelings**: Open up about your own emotions and experiences. Sharing your feelings can encourage reciprocity and create a more balanced and empathetic relationship.

7. **Cultivate Emotional Awareness**: Develop awareness of your own emotions and how they influence your interactions with others. Emotional awareness helps in understanding and empathizing with others.

8. **Practice Empathy in Daily Interactions**: Apply empathetic skills in everyday interactions with friends, family, and colleagues. Regular practice helps in reinforcing and enhancing your empathetic abilities.

**Overcoming Challenges in Developing Empathy**

1. **Overcoming Biases and Judgments**: Be aware of personal biases and judgments that may affect your ability to empathize. Challenge these biases and approach interactions with an open mind.

2. **Managing Emotional Overwhelm**: Empathy can sometimes lead to emotional overwhelm or burnout. Practice self-care and set boundaries to manage your emotional well-being while supporting others.

3. **Dealing with Defensive Reactions**: If you encounter defensiveness or resistance from others, approach the situation with patience and understanding. Avoid reacting defensively and maintain an empathetic stance.

4. **Balancing Empathy and Objectivity**: While empathy is important, maintaining objectivity is also crucial. Strive to balance empathy with practical solutions and rational decision-making.

5. **Addressing Cultural Differences**: Recognize and

respect cultural differences in emotional expression and communication styles. Be open to learning about and adapting to diverse perspectives.

**Practical Exercises to Enhance Empathy**

1. **Empathy Journaling**: Keep a journal to reflect on interactions and consider how others may have felt in various situations. Write about your observations and insights to develop a deeper understanding.

2. **Role-Playing Exercises**: Engage in role-playing exercises to practice perspective-taking and empathy. Assume different roles in various scenarios to experience different viewpoints.

3. **Empathy Mapping**: Create empathy maps to visualize and understand the feelings, thoughts, and needs of others. Use this tool to analyze and empathize with different perspectives.

4. **Empathy Exercises with Media**: Watch films, read books, or listen to stories that explore diverse human experiences. Reflect on the emotions and perspectives depicted and consider how they relate to your own life.

5. **Gratitude Practice**: Express gratitude to others for their support and understanding. Acknowledging and appreciating the positive aspects of your relationships enhances empathy and connection.

6. **Mindfulness Practice**: Incorporate mindfulness practices to enhance emotional awareness and empathy. Mindfulness helps in staying present and understanding others' emotions more deeply.

## Conclusion

Empathy plays a crucial role in building and sustaining intimate connections. By understanding and sharing the feelings of others, individuals can foster stronger relationships, enhance communication, and provide meaningful support. Developing empathetic skills requires active listening, perspective-taking, and emotional awareness. Overcoming challenges and practicing empathy in daily interactions contribute to deeper and more fulfilling connections.

In the next chapter, we will explore the impact of shared experiences on intimacy. We will discuss how engaging in activities together, creating memories, and nurturing common interests contribute to strengthening relationships. Join us as we continue to delve into the various dimensions of intimacy and their impact on our lives.

# CHAPTER 12: SEXUAL INTIMACY: MYTHS AND REALITIES

Sexual intimacy is a significant and often complex aspect of many relationships. It can deeply influence the connection between partners, yet it is frequently surrounded by myths and misconceptions that can impact expectations and experiences. This chapter addresses common myths about sexual intimacy and provides a realistic perspective on its role in relationships.

**Understanding Sexual Intimacy**

Sexual intimacy involves not only physical interaction but also emotional and psychological aspects. It encompasses a range of experiences, from physical pleasure to deeper emotional connections, and varies greatly from one relationship to another. It's essential to recognize that sexual intimacy is influenced by individual preferences, cultural norms, and personal values.

**Common Myths About Sexual Intimacy**

1. **Myth: Sexual Intimacy Equals Love**
   - **Reality:** While sexual intimacy can be an expression of love, it is not synonymous with it. Love is a deeper, multifaceted emotion that encompasses more than just sexual attraction. Relationships can be loving and fulfilling without sexual

intimacy, and sexual intimacy can exist without love.

2. **Myth: Good Sexual Intimacy Is Instinctive**
   - **Reality**: Sexual intimacy often requires communication, understanding, and effort. It is not always instinctive or automatic. Partners must discuss their needs, desires, and boundaries to ensure a satisfying sexual relationship.

3. **Myth: There Is a "Normal" Frequency for Sex**
   - **Reality**: There is no universal standard for how often couples should engage in sexual activity. Frequency varies greatly among couples and can be influenced by factors such as age, health, stress, and personal preferences. What matters is that both partners are satisfied with their sexual frequency and quality.

4. **Myth: Sexual Intimacy Should Be Spontaneous**
   - **Reality**: While spontaneity can be exciting, many couples benefit from planning and discussing their sexual needs. Regular communication and planning can enhance sexual intimacy and address any issues or concerns.

5. **Myth: Orgasm Is the Primary Goal of Sexual Intimacy**
   - **Reality**: Focusing solely on achieving orgasm can detract from the overall experience of sexual intimacy. The goal should be mutual pleasure, connection, and satisfaction, rather than just reaching climax.

6. **Myth: Sexual Compatibility Means Having the**

**Same Preferences**
- ◦ **Reality**: Sexual compatibility does not mean having identical preferences. It involves understanding and respecting each other's desires and finding ways to accommodate them. Compromise and communication play a crucial role in sexual compatibility.

7. **Myth: Sex Should Be Perfect Every Time**
   - ◦ **Reality**: Sexual experiences vary, and expecting perfection can create unnecessary pressure. Embrace the natural ebb and flow of sexual activity, and focus on connection and enjoyment rather than perfection.

8. **Myth: Sexual Intimacy Declines with Age**
   - ◦ **Reality**: Sexual intimacy can evolve with age but does not necessarily decline. Many older adults continue to have fulfilling and satisfying sexual experiences. Changes in sexual activity with age are often related to health, hormones, and relationship dynamics.

9. **Myth: Sexual Intimacy Is Only About Physical Touch**
   - ◦ **Reality**: Sexual intimacy encompasses emotional and psychological elements as well. Emotional connection, trust, and communication are crucial components of a fulfilling sexual relationship.

10. **Myth: A Lack of Sexual Desire Indicates Relationship Problems**
    - ◦ **Reality**: A decrease in sexual desire can result from various factors, including stress, health issues, and hormonal changes. It does not necessarily indicate relationship

problems. Open communication and seeking professional advice can help address these concerns.

## Realities of Sexual Intimacy

1. **Communication is Key**: Effective communication about sexual needs, preferences, and boundaries is essential for a satisfying sexual relationship. Discussing desires, experimenting with different approaches, and being open about concerns can enhance intimacy.

2. **Mutual Consent and Respect**: Sexual intimacy should always be consensual and based on mutual respect. Both partners must feel comfortable and willing to engage in sexual activities. Consent is an ongoing process and should be reaffirmed throughout the relationship.

3. **Emotional Connection Enhances Physical Intimacy**: Emotional connection and trust contribute significantly to sexual intimacy. Feeling emotionally secure and connected with your partner can enhance the overall sexual experience.

4. **Sexual Intimacy Can Be a Tool for Bonding**: Engaging in sexual intimacy can strengthen the bond between partners. It provides an opportunity for physical closeness, emotional expression, and shared pleasure.

5. **Exploration and Experimentation**: Exploring different aspects of sexual intimacy, such as new activities or techniques, can enhance the experience and maintain excitement in the relationship. Be open to experimentation and discuss preferences with your partner.

6. **Addressing Sexual Health**: Maintaining sexual

health is vital for a fulfilling sexual relationship. Regular check-ups, safe sex practices, and addressing any health concerns contribute to overall sexual well-being.

7. **Managing Expectations**: Understanding and managing expectations about sexual intimacy can prevent disappointment and frustration. Recognize that sexual experiences can vary and focus on mutual satisfaction rather than achieving specific outcomes.

8. **Seeking Professional Help**: If sexual intimacy issues arise, consider seeking help from a therapist or counselor. Professional guidance can assist in addressing concerns, improving communication, and enhancing sexual satisfaction.

**Practical Tips for Enhancing Sexual Intimacy**

1. **Create a Comfortable Environment**: Ensure that your sexual environment is comfortable and conducive to intimacy. Privacy, relaxation, and a positive atmosphere can enhance the experience.

2. **Prioritize Emotional Connection**: Build and maintain emotional intimacy with your partner through regular communication, shared experiences, and emotional support. A strong emotional connection enhances sexual intimacy.

3. **Experiment Together**: Explore new activities or approaches to sexual intimacy together. Discuss and try out different techniques, positions, or scenarios that interest both partners.

4. **Practice Open Communication**: Discuss sexual preferences, boundaries, and desires openly with your partner. Regular communication helps in understanding each other's needs and improving

sexual satisfaction.

5. **Focus on Foreplay**: Invest time in foreplay to enhance arousal and connection. Foreplay helps in building anticipation and increasing pleasure for both partners.

6. **Be Patient and Understanding**: Be patient with each other and approach sexual intimacy with an open and understanding mindset. Recognize that sexual experiences may vary and that mutual satisfaction is the goal.

7. **Prioritize Mutual Pleasure**: Focus on mutual pleasure rather than individual goals. Pay attention to each other's responses and work together to create a satisfying experience.

8. **Address Sexual Health Concerns**: Stay informed about sexual health and address any concerns with a healthcare professional. Regular check-ups and safe practices contribute to overall sexual well-being.

## Conclusion

Sexual intimacy is a multifaceted aspect of relationships that involves more than just physical interaction. By addressing common myths and embracing the realities of sexual intimacy, individuals can foster deeper connections and enhance their sexual experiences. Effective communication, mutual consent, emotional connection, and exploration are key to a fulfilling sexual relationship. Understanding and managing expectations, maintaining sexual health, and seeking professional help when needed contribute to a positive and satisfying sexual experience.

In the next chapter, we will explore the concept of intellectual intimacy and its role in relationships. We will discuss how sharing ideas, engaging in stimulating conversations, and appreciating each other's intellect contribute to deepening connections. Join us as we continue our journey through the dimensions of intimacy and their impact on our lives.

# CHAPTER 13: THE POWER OF NON-SEXUAL TOUCH

Non-sexual touch, including actions such as hugging, holding hands, and cuddling, often holds a profound impact on relationships. While these forms of touch are not directly related to sexual activity, they play a crucial role in fostering intimacy and enhancing relationship satisfaction. This chapter explores the benefits of non-sexual touch and its significance in building and maintaining strong, emotional connections.

**Understanding Non-Sexual Touch**

Non-sexual touch refers to physical interactions that are not intended to be sexual in nature but serve to convey affection, support, and connection. Examples include:

- **Hugging**: An embrace that provides comfort and emotional support.

- **Holding Hands**: A gesture of closeness and solidarity.

- **Cuddling**: A form of physical closeness that promotes warmth and security.

- **Gentle Touches**: Casual touches on the arm, shoulder, or back that convey warmth and care.

**The Benefits of Non-Sexual Touch**

1. **Strengthening Emotional Bonds**: Non-sexual touch

helps to strengthen emotional bonds between individuals. It provides a sense of connection and closeness that reinforces the relationship.

2. **Reducing Stress and Anxiety**: Physical touch has been shown to reduce levels of stress and anxiety. It triggers the release of oxytocin, a hormone associated with bonding and relaxation, which can lower cortisol levels and promote a sense of calm.

3. **Enhancing Feelings of Security**: Non-sexual touch can create a feeling of safety and security. It provides reassurance and comfort, making individuals feel valued and cared for.

4. **Improving Relationship Satisfaction**: Regular non-sexual touch contributes to overall relationship satisfaction. It helps maintain a sense of closeness and affection, which is essential for a fulfilling relationship.

5. **Encouraging Positive Communication**: Physical touch can enhance communication by expressing emotions that words might not fully convey. It adds a layer of non-verbal communication that can strengthen understanding and connection.

6. **Promoting Physical Health**: Non-sexual touch can have positive effects on physical health. It has been linked to lower blood pressure, improved immune function, and better overall well-being.

7. **Supporting Emotional Recovery**: During times of distress or emotional upheaval, non-sexual touch can offer comfort and support. It provides a tangible expression of care and empathy that can aid in emotional recovery.

8. **Building Trust and Intimacy**: Regular non-sexual touch helps build trust and intimacy by creating

opportunities for closeness and connection. It reinforces the emotional bond between partners and enhances overall relationship quality.

**Types of Non-Sexual Touch and Their Impact**

1. **Hugging**: Hugs are a powerful form of non-sexual touch that can provide comfort and emotional support. They promote a sense of connection and are often used to convey empathy and reassurance.

   - **Benefits of Hugging**: Hugs can reduce stress, boost mood, and increase feelings of security. They are often used to celebrate achievements, offer comfort during challenging times, and reinforce emotional bonds.

2. **Holding Hands**: Holding hands is a simple yet meaningful gesture that signifies closeness and solidarity. It can be used to express affection, support, and companionship.

   - **Benefits of Holding Hands**: This gesture can enhance feelings of connection and intimacy. It is often used in public settings to show unity and support, and in private moments to reinforce emotional closeness.

3. **Cuddling**: Cuddling involves physical closeness and can provide a sense of warmth and security. It is often associated with feelings of comfort and emotional connection.

   - **Benefits of Cuddling**: Cuddling promotes relaxation and reduces stress. It can strengthen emotional bonds and provide a sense of safety and reassurance.

4. **Gentle Touches**: Casual touches, such as a pat on the back or a gentle touch on the arm, can convey affection and care without being intrusive.

- ◦ **Benefits of Gentle Touches**: These small gestures can enhance feelings of connection and support. They provide opportunities for physical closeness and express care in everyday interactions.

5. **Playful Touches**: Playful touches, such as tickling or light-hearted nudges, can foster a sense of fun and joy in the relationship.
    - ◦ **Benefits of Playful Touches**: These interactions can create shared moments of laughter and enjoyment, strengthening the emotional bond and enhancing relationship satisfaction.

**Integrating Non-Sexual Touch into Daily Life**

1. **Make It a Habit**: Incorporate non-sexual touch into daily interactions. Simple gestures like hugging, holding hands, or offering a gentle touch can reinforce emotional connection and affection.

2. **Be Attuned to Your Partner's Preferences**: Pay attention to your partner's comfort level and preferences regarding touch. Respect their boundaries and adjust your approach based on their responses.

3. **Use Touch to Communicate Emotion**: Use non-sexual touch to express emotions that may be difficult to articulate with words. Physical contact can convey support, love, and empathy.

4. **Create Rituals of Touch**: Establish rituals or routines involving non-sexual touch, such as a goodnight hug or a morning embrace. These rituals can enhance feelings of connection and consistency.

5. **Address Touch Deprivation**: If either partner feels deprived of touch, address this concern openly.

Discuss ways to incorporate more non-sexual touch into the relationship to meet both partners' needs.

6. **Practice Mindful Touch**: Be present and intentional when engaging in non-sexual touch. Focus on the emotional and physical sensations to enhance the impact and connection.

7. **Be Responsive to Changing Needs**: Recognize that needs and preferences regarding touch can change over time. Be open to discussing and adapting to these changes to maintain a strong emotional bond.

**Overcoming Challenges Related to Non-Sexual Touch**

1. **Addressing Comfort Levels**: Some individuals may have personal or cultural reasons for discomfort with physical touch. Approach these concerns with sensitivity and respect, and find alternative ways to express affection.

2. **Managing Physical Boundaries**: Ensure that non-sexual touch respects personal boundaries and preferences. Avoid pressuring your partner into physical contact if they are uncomfortable.

3. **Navigating Changes in Touch Needs**: Changes in physical touch needs may occur due to factors such as stress, health issues, or relationship dynamics. Communicate openly about these changes and find ways to adapt.

4. **Balancing Physical and Emotional Needs**: Ensure that non-sexual touch complements other aspects of the relationship, such as emotional support and communication. Balance physical affection with other forms of connection.

## Conclusion

Non-sexual touch is a powerful and meaningful way to foster intimacy and strengthen relationships. By incorporating gestures such as hugging, holding hands, and cuddling into daily interactions, individuals can enhance emotional bonds, reduce stress, and improve overall relationship satisfaction. Understanding the benefits of non-sexual touch and being attuned to each other's preferences can lead to a deeper and more fulfilling connection.

In the next chapter, we will explore the role of intellectual intimacy in relationships. We will discuss how sharing ideas, engaging in stimulating conversations, and appreciating each other's intellect contribute to deepening connections. Join us as we continue our exploration of the various dimensions of intimacy and their impact on our lives.

# CHAPTER 14: INTIMACY IN LONG-DISTANCE RELATIONSHIPS

Long-distance relationships (LDRs) can be both rewarding and challenging. Despite the physical separation, maintaining intimacy is crucial for sustaining a strong emotional connection. This chapter offers practical advice for sustaining intimacy across distances, highlighting strategies to overcome the unique obstacles faced by couples who are apart.

**Understanding Long-Distance Relationships**

A long-distance relationship is defined by the physical separation of partners, which can arise from various circumstances such as work, education, family obligations, or travel. Despite the distance, the goal is to maintain a meaningful connection and nurture the relationship.

**Challenges of Long-Distance Relationships**

1. **Lack of Physical Presence**: One of the most significant challenges is the absence of physical closeness, which can affect the ability to engage in shared activities and offer physical comfort.

2. **Communication Barriers**: Misunderstandings can arise more easily through text or phone calls due to the lack of non-verbal cues. Managing effective

communication becomes crucial.

3. **Time Zone Differences**: Coordinating schedules and finding overlapping times for communication can be challenging when partners are in different time zones.

4. **Emotional Strain**: The separation can lead to feelings of loneliness, frustration, or insecurity, which may affect the emotional well-being of both partners.

5. **Building and Maintaining Trust**: Trust is essential in any relationship but becomes even more critical in a long-distance relationship. The lack of daily interaction requires a higher level of trust and assurance.

**Strategies for Maintaining Intimacy**

1. **Effective Communication**:
    - **Scheduled Check-Ins**: Set regular times to communicate through phone calls, video chats, or messages. Consistent check-ins help maintain connection and prevent feelings of neglect.

    - **Open and Honest Dialogue**: Discuss your feelings, concerns, and needs openly. Honest communication helps build trust and prevents misunderstandings.

2. **Emotional Support**:
    - **Share Daily Experiences**: Keep each other updated on daily activities, achievements, and challenges. Sharing these experiences helps maintain a sense of closeness and involvement in each other's lives.

    - **Offer Reassurance**: Regularly express affection and reassurance to each other. Words of affirmation and support can strengthen emotional bonds and alleviate insecurities.

3.  **Creative Ways to Connect**:
    - **Virtual Dates**: Plan virtual dates where you can watch movies, play games, or have dinner together over video calls. Creative activities help simulate shared experiences and foster intimacy.

    - **Send Care Packages**: Surprise each other with care packages or handwritten letters. Physical tokens of affection can provide comfort and remind each other of your love.

4.  **Setting Goals and Expectations**:
    - **Discuss Future Plans**: Talk about future plans and goals for the relationship. Having a shared vision for the future can provide motivation and hope.

    - **Establish Boundaries**: Clearly define boundaries and expectations regarding communication, social activities, and interactions with others. This helps prevent misunderstandings and conflicts.

5.  **Maintaining Physical Connection**:
    - **Exchange Personal Items**: Share personal items like clothing or keepsakes that hold sentimental value. These items can provide comfort and a sense of closeness.

    - **Plan Visits**: Schedule regular visits whenever possible. Face-to-face interactions are crucial for maintaining physical and emotional intimacy.

6.  **Embrace Technology**:
    - **Use Communication Tools**: Utilize various

communication tools such as video calls, messaging apps, and social media to stay connected. Explore different platforms to find what works best for you.

- **Share Media**: Exchange photos, videos, and voice messages to maintain a sense of presence and involvement in each other's lives.

7. **Build Trust and Transparency**:
    - **Be Transparent**: Share your feelings and experiences openly, and encourage your partner to do the same. Transparency fosters trust and prevents feelings of isolation.
    - **Address Concerns Promptly**: Address any concerns or issues as they arise. Promptly addressing problems can prevent them from escalating and affecting the relationship.

8. **Focus on the Positive**:
    - **Celebrate Milestones**: Celebrate special occasions, anniversaries, and achievements together. Acknowledge and appreciate each other's efforts and accomplishments.
    - **Stay Positive**: Focus on the positive aspects of the relationship and the benefits of the distance. Emphasize the strength and growth of the relationship despite the challenges.

9. **Self-Care and Independence**:
    - **Prioritize Self-Care**: Take care of your physical and emotional well-being. Engaging in activities that bring you joy and fulfillment can help you stay positive and resilient.

- **Maintain Independence**: Cultivate your own hobbies, interests, and social connections. Maintaining independence allows you to grow individually while sustaining a strong relationship.

## Overcoming Challenges

1. **Dealing with Loneliness**: Combat feelings of loneliness by staying connected with friends and family. Engage in activities that bring you joy and provide a sense of fulfillment.

2. **Managing Jealousy and Insecurity**: Address feelings of jealousy or insecurity through open communication and reassurance. Building trust and understanding can help alleviate these concerns.

3. **Coordinating Time Zones**: Plan communication around overlapping time zones. Use scheduling tools or apps to find convenient times for both partners.

4. **Handling Disagreements**: Resolve conflicts with empathy and understanding. Focus on finding solutions and maintaining a positive outlook on the relationship.

5. **Navigating Life Changes**: Adjust to changes in personal or professional life by communicating openly and supporting each other through transitions.

## Conclusion

Maintaining intimacy in a long-distance relationship requires effort, creativity, and commitment. By employing strategies such as effective communication, emotional support, and creative ways to connect, couples can nurture their bond despite the physical separation. Building trust, managing expectations, and focusing on the positive aspects of the relationship contribute to a fulfilling and resilient connection.

In the next chapter, we will explore the concept of intellectual intimacy and its role in relationships. We will discuss how sharing ideas, engaging in stimulating conversations, and appreciating each other's intellect contribute to deepening connections. Join us as we continue our journey through the dimensions of intimacy and their impact on our lives.

# CHAPTER 15: CULTURAL PERSPECTIVES ON INTIMACY

Intimacy is a multifaceted concept that is deeply influenced by cultural norms and values. Different cultures have unique ways of perceiving, expressing, and experiencing intimacy, reflecting their diverse social, historical, and psychological contexts. This chapter explores how various cultures approach intimacy, highlighting the richness and diversity of intimate practices around the world.

## Understanding Cultural Influences on Intimacy

Culture profoundly shapes our understanding of intimacy, influencing how we connect with others, express affection, and build relationships. Cultural norms dictate the acceptable ways to demonstrate closeness and affection, as well as the boundaries and expectations associated with intimate interactions.

## Cultural Variations in Expressing Intimacy

1. **Collectivist Cultures:**
   - **Overview:** In collectivist cultures, such as those in many Asian, African, and Latin American societies, group harmony and familial ties are highly valued. Intimacy

is often expressed through actions that reinforce group cohesion and familial responsibilities.

- **Expressions of Intimacy**: Intimacy in collectivist cultures is frequently demonstrated through acts of service, respect for elders, and adherence to family roles. Physical touch may be less overt, with emotional support and shared responsibilities taking precedence.

2. **Individualist Cultures**:
- **Overview**: Individualist cultures, such as those in many Western societies, emphasize personal autonomy and self-expression. Intimacy is often associated with personal fulfillment and individual emotional needs.

- **Expressions of Intimacy**: In individualist cultures, intimacy is commonly expressed through verbal communication, physical affection, and personal sharing. Romantic relationships may focus on personal compatibility and emotional connection, with a greater emphasis on expressing feelings and desires.

3. **Communal Cultures**:
- **Overview**: Communal cultures, found in various parts of the Middle East and Africa, prioritize communal living and shared experiences. Intimacy is often built through collective activities and community bonds.

- **Expressions of Intimacy**: Intimacy in communal cultures may involve frequent communal gatherings, shared meals, and group rituals. Physical touch and emotional support are often integral to community life, reinforcing social ties and mutual care.

4. **Hierarchical Cultures**:
   - **Overview**: Hierarchical cultures, prevalent in certain Asian societies, emphasize social hierarchy and respect for authority. Intimacy is often structured around social roles and obligations.
   - **Expressions of Intimacy**: In hierarchical cultures, intimacy is expressed through adherence to social norms, respect for elders, and fulfillment of familial duties. Relationships may be characterized by formal expressions of affection and a focus on maintaining social harmony.

5. **Romantic Cultures**:
   - **Overview**: Romantic cultures, such as those in France and Italy, place a high value on romantic love and passionate expression. Intimacy is often intertwined with romantic ideals and emotional depth.
   - **Expressions of Intimacy**: In romantic cultures, intimacy is frequently demonstrated through overt physical affection, poetic expressions of love, and romantic gestures. Emotional connection and personal fulfillment are central to intimate relationships.

## Case Studies: Cultural Perspectives on Intimacy

1. **Japanese Culture**:
   - **Overview**: Japanese culture values subtlety and indirect communication. Intimacy is often expressed through non-verbal cues and shared experiences rather than overt

declarations of affection.

- **Practices**: In Japan, couples may express intimacy through actions such as thoughtful gestures, gift-giving, and participating in shared activities. Public displays of affection are generally reserved for private settings.

2. **Indian Culture**:

- **Overview**: Indian culture places a strong emphasis on family and community. Intimacy within relationships is often influenced by cultural and familial expectations.

- **Practices**: Intimacy in India may be expressed through acts of service, respect for elders, and participation in family rituals. Romantic relationships often involve familial approval and adherence to traditional values.

3. **Brazilian Culture**:

- **Overview**: Brazilian culture is known for its warm and expressive nature. Intimacy is frequently conveyed through physical touch and lively social interactions.

- **Practices**: In Brazil, intimacy is often expressed through hugging, kissing on the cheek, and engaging in vibrant social gatherings. Emotional connection is reinforced through enthusiastic and affectionate interactions.

4. **Middle Eastern Culture**:

- **Overview**: Middle Eastern cultures often emphasize communal living and respect for tradition. Intimacy is expressed through adherence to social norms and family-oriented values.

- **Practices**: In Middle Eastern cultures, intimacy may involve family gatherings, shared meals, and maintaining strong familial bonds. Physical touch is typically reserved for close family members and may be less common in public.

5. **Swedish Culture**:
   - **Overview**: Swedish culture values personal space and equality. Intimacy is often expressed through mutual respect and understanding rather than overt physical affection.

   - **Practices**: In Sweden, intimacy is demonstrated through thoughtful communication, respecting personal boundaries, and maintaining a balanced approach to affection. Emotional support is prioritized in relationships.

## The Impact of Globalization on Intimacy

Globalization has led to increased cultural exchange and interaction, influencing how intimacy is perceived and practiced across different societies. As cultures intersect, individuals may adopt and adapt various practices, leading to a blending of intimate traditions and norms.

1. **Cultural Exchange**: Exposure to different cultures through media, travel, and migration has led to a greater understanding and incorporation of diverse intimate practices. This exchange can enrich relationships and broaden perspectives on intimacy.

2. **Hybrid Practices**: In multicultural societies, individuals may develop hybrid practices that blend

elements from different cultural traditions. This blending can create unique expressions of intimacy that reflect a combination of cultural influences.

3. **Challenges and Opportunities**: Globalization presents both challenges and opportunities for maintaining cultural traditions while embracing new ways of connecting. Individuals may navigate these dynamics by balancing traditional values with contemporary practices.

## Conclusion

Cultural perspectives on intimacy reflect the diverse ways in which individuals connect with one another and express affection. Understanding these cultural variations enhances our appreciation of the rich tapestry of intimate practices around the world. By exploring different cultural approaches to intimacy, we gain insight into the universal and culturally specific aspects of human connection.

In the next chapter, we will examine the role of intimacy in personal growth and self-discovery. We will explore how intimate relationships contribute to our development, self-awareness, and overall well-being. Join us as we continue our exploration of the dimensions of intimacy and their impact on our lives.

# CHAPTER 16:
# TECHNOLOGY
# AND INTIMACY

Technology has dramatically transformed the landscape of human connection, reshaping how we build and maintain intimate relationships. From instant messaging to video calls and social media, technology has opened new avenues for staying connected. However, it also presents challenges that can impact the quality and nature of intimacy. This chapter explores the effects of technology on intimacy, examining both its benefits and potential drawbacks.

**The Evolution of Technological Communication**

1. **Instant Messaging and Texting**:
   - **Overview**: Instant messaging and texting have revolutionized communication, allowing individuals to stay in touch regardless of geographical distance. These technologies offer convenience and immediacy, enabling real-time exchanges of thoughts and feelings.

   - **Benefits**: Instant messaging facilitates quick and frequent communication, making it easier to share daily experiences, maintain connections, and express support. It also allows for asynchronous conversations, which can accommodate different schedules and time zones.

- **Drawbacks**: Text-based communication lacks non-verbal cues, which can lead to misunderstandings and reduced emotional depth. The brevity and informality of texting may sometimes undermine the quality of intimate exchanges.

2. **Video Calls and Virtual Meetings**:
   - **Overview**: Video calls and virtual meetings provide a more immersive form of communication, allowing individuals to see and hear each other in real time. These technologies bridge the gap between face-to-face and digital interactions.

   - **Benefits**: Video calls enhance emotional connection by offering visual and auditory cues that text alone cannot provide. They facilitate face-to-face conversations, helping to maintain a sense of presence and closeness despite physical separation.

   - **Drawbacks**: Technical issues such as poor connectivity or lag can disrupt communication and lead to frustration. Additionally, the need for scheduled video calls may limit spontaneity and natural interaction.

3. **Social Media**:
   - **Overview**: Social media platforms have become integral to how people connect and share their lives. They offer various tools for maintaining relationships, from sharing updates to participating in group discussions.

   - **Benefits**: Social media allows for broad and

diverse interactions, enabling individuals to connect with a wide network of friends and family. It also provides a platform for expressing support, celebrating milestones, and staying informed about others' lives.

- **Drawbacks**: Social media can lead to superficial connections and comparisons, which may impact self-esteem and relationship satisfaction. It also poses privacy risks and can contribute to the phenomenon of "performative intimacy," where online interactions may lack genuine depth.

4. **Dating Apps and Online Platforms**:
   - **Overview**: Dating apps and online platforms have transformed the way people meet and form romantic relationships. These technologies offer new methods for discovering and connecting with potential partners.

   - **Benefits**: Dating apps provide access to a larger pool of potential partners and facilitate connections based on shared interests and preferences. They also offer convenience and flexibility in initiating and maintaining romantic interactions.

   - **Drawbacks**: The online dating experience can sometimes lead to superficial judgments based on profiles and photos. The anonymity and distance provided by online platforms may also contribute to misrepresentation and unrealistic expectations.

## The Impact of Technology on Intimacy

1. **Enhanced Connectivity**:
   - **Overview**: Technology enables individuals to stay connected across distances, fostering relationships that might otherwise be challenging to maintain. It facilitates regular communication and emotional support.
   - **Examples**: Long-distance couples can use video calls to share moments and discuss their day. Friends separated by geographical boundaries can use social media to stay updated and involved in each other's lives.

2. **Increased Accessibility**:
   - **Overview**: Technology offers greater accessibility to communication tools, making it easier to maintain connections regardless of physical location. This accessibility can strengthen relationships and provide support during challenging times.
   - **Examples**: Virtual support groups and online counseling services offer valuable resources for individuals seeking emotional support and connection.

3. **Altered Dynamics of Intimacy**:
   - **Overview**: The prevalence of digital communication has changed the dynamics of intimacy, influencing how people connect and express affection. Technology can both facilitate and hinder the development of deep, meaningful relationships.
   - **Examples**: While digital communication allows for constant contact, it may also reduce opportunities for spontaneous, face-

to-face interactions that contribute to emotional closeness.

4. **Potential for Miscommunication**:
   - **Overview**: The absence of non-verbal cues in text-based communication can lead to misinterpretations and misunderstandings. This potential for miscommunication can impact the quality of intimate exchanges.
   - **Examples**: Ambiguities in text messages or emails can lead to confusion or conflict, requiring additional effort to clarify intentions and emotions.

5. **Privacy and Boundaries**:
   - **Overview**: Technology raises concerns about privacy and boundaries, particularly in the context of sharing personal information and maintaining digital presence. Managing these aspects is crucial for protecting intimacy and trust.
   - **Examples**: The sharing of private moments on social media or the use of tracking apps can impact personal privacy and relationship boundaries.

## Strategies for Balancing Technology and Intimacy

1. **Prioritize Face-to-Face Interaction**:
   - **Overview**: Whenever possible, prioritize in-person interactions to foster deeper emotional connections. Face-to-face communication offers richer, more nuanced exchanges that technology may not fully replicate.
   - **Tips**: Schedule regular visits, plan face-to-face activities, and engage in spontaneous

interactions that enhance intimacy.

2. **Set Communication Boundaries**:
   - **Overview**: Establish clear boundaries for digital communication to maintain balance and prevent technology from encroaching on personal space. Respect each other's need for downtime and privacy.
   - **Tips**: Define times for phone calls and online communication, and set limits on screen time to avoid digital overload.

3. **Practice Mindful Communication**:
   - **Overview**: Approach digital communication with mindfulness, being aware of the potential for miscommunication and the importance of clarity. Use thoughtful language and verify intentions when needed.
   - **Tips**: Use video calls for sensitive discussions, and take the time to compose thoughtful messages that reflect your true feelings.

4. **Safeguard Privacy**:
   - **Overview**: Protect personal privacy and maintain boundaries by being cautious about sharing information online and using privacy settings effectively.
   - **Tips**: Avoid oversharing personal details on social media, and be mindful of the digital footprint you create.

5. **Foster Genuine Connections**:
   - **Overview**: Focus on building genuine connections by engaging in meaningful conversations and expressing authentic

emotions. Prioritize quality over quantity in digital interactions.

- ◦ **Tips**: Share personal experiences, offer support, and celebrate milestones together to strengthen emotional bonds.

6. **Balance Digital and Physical Presence**:
   - ◦ **Overview**: Strive to balance digital interactions with physical presence, ensuring that technology complements rather than replaces personal connections.
   - ◦ **Tips**: Use technology to enhance and support in-person interactions, rather than relying solely on digital communication.

## Conclusion

Technology has significantly impacted the way we connect and build intimacy, offering both opportunities and challenges. While digital tools facilitate communication and enhance connectivity, they also present potential drawbacks that can affect the quality of intimate relationships. By understanding these dynamics and employing strategies to balance technology with personal connection, individuals can navigate the complexities of modern intimacy and cultivate meaningful relationships.

In the next chapter, we will explore the role of emotional intelligence in intimacy. We will discuss how self-awareness, empathy, and emotional regulation contribute to deepening connections and enhancing relationship satisfaction. Join us as we continue our journey through the dimensions of intimacy and their impact on our lives.

# CHAPTER 17: INTIMACY IN THE DIGITAL AGE

The digital age has revolutionized how we interact, offering new platforms and tools for connecting with others. Social media, online dating, and virtual communication have become integral to modern relationships, providing both opportunities and challenges for intimacy. This chapter explores how these digital innovations have transformed intimate relationships, examining their impact on connection, communication, and relationship dynamics.

**Social Media and Intimacy**

Social media platforms have become ubiquitous in our daily lives, shaping how we connect with friends, family, and romantic partners. These platforms offer new ways to share experiences, express affection, and stay engaged with others.

1. **Benefits of Social Media for Intimacy**:
   - **Constant Connection**: Social media allows for continuous interaction, enabling individuals to stay in touch and share updates in real time. This constant connection can help maintain relationships and provide emotional support.
   - **Sharing and Celebrating**: Platforms like Facebook, Instagram, and Twitter offer opportunities to celebrate milestones,

share personal achievements, and express gratitude, reinforcing bonds and fostering a sense of closeness.

- **Building Community**: Social media facilitates the creation of online communities and support networks, allowing individuals to connect with like-minded people and share experiences that enhance their sense of belonging.

2. **Challenges of Social Media for Intimacy**:
    - **Superficial Connections**: Social media interactions can sometimes be superficial, focusing on likes, shares, and comments rather than meaningful conversations. This can lead to a lack of depth in relationships.

    - **Comparison and Envy**: Exposure to curated portrayals of others' lives can lead to comparisons and feelings of inadequacy, impacting self-esteem and relationship satisfaction.

    - **Privacy Concerns**: Sharing personal information and relationship details on social media can raise privacy issues and lead to conflicts over what should be publicly disclosed.

## Online Dating and Romantic Intimacy

Online dating platforms have transformed how people meet and form romantic relationships, offering new opportunities for connection while also presenting unique challenges.

1. **Benefits of Online Dating**:
    - **Expanded Reach**: Online dating apps and websites provide access to a larger pool of potential partners, allowing individuals

to connect with people they might not encounter in their everyday lives.

- **Convenience**: Dating apps offer a convenient way to initiate and maintain romantic connections, providing flexibility in managing interactions and schedules.

- **Filtered Matches**: Many platforms use algorithms and preferences to match individuals based on shared interests, values, and goals, potentially increasing the likelihood of compatibility.

2. **Challenges of Online Dating**:

- **Surface-Level Judgments**: Online dating often relies on profiles and photos, which can lead to superficial judgments and may not accurately reflect a person's true character or compatibility.

- **Misrepresentation**: The anonymity of online dating can lead to misrepresentation and unrealistic expectations, making it challenging to establish genuine connections.

- **Overwhelm and Choice Paralysis**: The vast number of options available on dating platforms can be overwhelming, leading to choice paralysis and difficulty in making meaningful connections.

## Virtual Communication and Intimacy

Virtual communication tools, such as video calls, messaging apps, and virtual reality, have expanded the ways we interact with others, influencing how we experience and maintain intimacy.

1. **Benefits of Virtual Communication**:

- **Visual and Auditory Cues**: Video calls provide visual and auditory cues that enhance emotional connection, making conversations more personal and engaging compared to text alone.
- **Flexibility and Accessibility**: Virtual communication allows for flexible scheduling and accessibility, enabling individuals to connect with loved ones regardless of geographical distance.
- **Enhanced Interaction**: Virtual reality and other immersive technologies offer new ways to interact and engage with others, creating shared experiences and activities that can strengthen bonds.

2. **Challenges of Virtual Communication**:
   - **Technical Issues**: Technical difficulties, such as poor connectivity or hardware limitations, can disrupt communication and impact the quality of interactions.
   - **Screen Fatigue**: The increased use of screens for communication can lead to screen fatigue and reduced engagement, impacting the overall experience of intimacy.
   - **Reduced Spontaneity**: Virtual communication often requires scheduling and planning, which can reduce the spontaneity and natural flow of interactions.

## Navigating Intimacy in the Digital Age

1. **Balancing Digital and In-Person Interaction**:
   - **Overview**: While digital tools offer valuable ways to connect, it is important to

balance online interactions with in-person experiences to maintain the depth and richness of relationships.

- **Tips**: Prioritize face-to-face meetings when possible, use digital tools to complement rather than replace in-person interactions, and schedule regular quality time with loved ones.

2. **Maintaining Authenticity and Depth**:
   - **Overview**: To foster genuine connections, focus on authenticity and depth in digital interactions. Avoid superficial exchanges and strive for meaningful conversations that reflect true emotions and intentions.
   - **Tips**: Be honest and transparent in your online communications, actively listen to others, and engage in conversations that explore deeper aspects of your relationships.

3. **Setting Boundaries and Managing Privacy**:
   - **Overview**: Establish clear boundaries for digital communication and protect your privacy to ensure a healthy balance between online and offline aspects of your relationships.
   - **Tips**: Define limits for social media sharing, manage privacy settings effectively, and communicate openly with partners and friends about digital boundaries.

4. **Addressing Digital Challenges**:
   - **Overview**: Recognize and address challenges associated with digital communication, such as miscommunication and technical issues, to enhance the quality of your interactions.

- ○ **Tips**: Use video calls for important discussions, clarify intentions when needed, and address technical problems promptly to ensure smooth communication.

## Conclusion

The digital age has brought both opportunities and challenges for intimacy, reshaping how we connect and interact with others. While social media, online dating, and virtual communication offer new ways to build and maintain relationships, they also present unique issues that can impact the quality and depth of intimacy. By understanding these dynamics and employing strategies to navigate the digital landscape, individuals can cultivate meaningful connections and enhance their relationships in the modern world.

In the next chapter, we will explore the role of emotional intelligence in fostering intimate connections. We will discuss how self-awareness, empathy, and emotional regulation contribute to developing deeper, more fulfilling relationships. Join us as we continue our journey through the dimensions of intimacy and their impact on our lives.

# CHAPTER 18:
# THE IMPACT OF
# SOCIAL MEDIA

Social media has woven itself into the fabric of modern life, offering unprecedented ways to connect with others. While it provides valuable tools for communication and relationship maintenance, it also poses challenges that can impact the quality and nature of intimacy. This chapter examines how social media affects relationships, exploring both its positive and negative impacts and offering strategies for balancing online interactions with face-to-face connections.

**The Positive Impacts of Social Media on Intimacy**

1. **Enhanced Connectivity:**
    - **Overview:** Social media platforms allow individuals to stay connected with friends, family, and partners, regardless of geographical distance. This constant connectivity can help maintain relationships and provide emotional support.

    - **Examples:** Sharing daily updates, photos, and messages can keep loved ones informed about each other's lives. Virtual check-ins and interactions through platforms like Facebook, Instagram, and Twitter can strengthen bonds and foster a sense of closeness.

2. **Opportunities for Expressing Affection**:
   - **Overview**: Social media provides numerous ways to express affection and appreciation. Public posts, direct messages, and shared content can convey love, support, and recognition.
   - **Examples**: Celebrating milestones such as birthdays or anniversaries on social media can enhance relationship satisfaction and reinforce positive feelings. Public declarations of support and gratitude can also strengthen emotional connections.

3. **Support and Community Building**:
   - **Overview**: Social media offers platforms for creating and participating in support networks and online communities. These communities can provide valuable resources, encouragement, and a sense of belonging.
   - **Examples**: Joining groups related to personal interests or challenges can connect individuals with like-minded people and offer emotional support. Online forums and support groups can also provide a sense of community and shared experience.

4. **Facilitating Reconnection**:
   - **Overview**: Social media can help people reconnect with old friends and acquaintances, rekindling relationships that may have faded over time.
   - **Examples**: Finding and reaching out to former classmates, colleagues, or family members through social media platforms

can revive past connections and rekindle relationships.

**The Negative Impacts of Social Media on Intimacy**

1. **Superficial Interactions**:
    - **Overview**: Social media interactions can sometimes be superficial, focusing on likes, shares, and comments rather than meaningful conversations. This can lead to a lack of depth in relationships.
    - **Examples**: The brevity and informality of social media interactions may not allow for the in-depth discussions and emotional exchanges that contribute to true intimacy.

2. **Comparison and Envy**:
    - **Overview**: Exposure to curated and idealized portrayals of others' lives on social media can lead to comparisons and feelings of inadequacy. This can negatively impact self-esteem and relationship satisfaction.
    - **Examples**: Seeing others' highlights and achievements may lead to envy or self-doubt, which can strain relationships and diminish personal happiness.

3. **Privacy Concerns**:
    - **Overview**: Sharing personal information and relationship details on social media can raise privacy issues and lead to conflicts over what should be publicly disclosed.
    - **Examples**: Disagreements over the sharing of private moments or personal details on social media can cause tension between partners or friends.

4. **Time Management and Digital Overload**:

- ◦ **Overview**: Excessive time spent on social media can lead to digital overload and interfere with real-life interactions. Balancing online engagement with face-to-face relationships is essential for maintaining intimacy.
- ◦ **Examples**: Spending significant time on social media at the expense of in-person interactions can lead to reduced quality time with loved ones and impact relationship satisfaction.

## Balancing Online and Offline Interactions

1. **Prioritize In-Person Connection**:
    - ◦ **Overview**: While social media provides valuable tools for staying connected, it is essential to prioritize in-person interactions to maintain the depth and richness of relationships.
    - ◦ **Tips**: Schedule regular face-to-face meetings, engage in shared activities, and make time for spontaneous interactions that enhance intimacy.

2. **Set Boundaries for Social Media Use**:
    - ◦ **Overview**: Establishing boundaries for social media use can help manage digital overload and prevent it from interfering with personal relationships.
    - ◦ **Tips**: Define specific times for social media use, avoid checking devices during important moments, and communicate openly with partners and friends about digital boundaries.

3. **Focus on Authentic Engagement**:

- **Overview**: Strive for authenticity in online interactions by engaging in meaningful conversations and expressing genuine emotions. Avoid superficial exchanges and prioritize quality over quantity.

- **Tips**: Share personal experiences, offer heartfelt support, and engage in discussions that reflect your true feelings and intentions.

4. **Be Mindful of Privacy and Boundaries**:
   - **Overview**: Protect your privacy and maintain boundaries by being cautious about sharing personal information and relationship details on social media.

   - **Tips**: Use privacy settings effectively, avoid oversharing sensitive information, and respect others' privacy in your online interactions.

5. **Manage Social Media Expectations**:
   - **Overview**: Recognize that social media may not fully capture the complexity of relationships and that online interactions can sometimes differ from real-life experiences.

   - **Tips**: Set realistic expectations for social media engagement, and focus on nurturing relationships through various forms of communication, both online and offline.

## Conclusion

Social media has become a powerful tool for connecting with others, offering both opportunities and challenges for intimacy. While it enhances connectivity, provides ways to express affection, and supports community building, it also presents issues such as superficial interactions, comparison, and privacy concerns. By understanding the impact of social media and implementing strategies to balance online and offline interactions, individuals can navigate the complexities of digital relationships and foster deeper, more meaningful connections.

In the next chapter, we will explore the role of emotional intelligence in enhancing intimacy. We will discuss how self-awareness, empathy, and emotional regulation contribute to developing and maintaining fulfilling relationships. Join us as we continue our exploration of the dimensions of intimacy and their significance in our lives.

# CHAPTER 19: INTIMACY AND MENTAL HEALTH

Intimacy is not just a vital component of relationships but also closely tied to mental health. Positive, supportive relationships play a crucial role in emotional well-being, offering psychological resilience and contributing to overall mental health. This chapter explores the connection between intimacy and mental health, examining how intimate connections influence psychological resilience and discussing the benefits of nurturing meaningful relationships for mental wellness.

**The Connection Between Intimacy and Mental Health**

1. **Emotional Support and Well-Being**:
   - **Overview**: Intimate relationships provide a source of emotional support, which can significantly impact mental health. Having someone to confide in, share experiences with, and receive comfort from can enhance emotional resilience and reduce feelings of loneliness and isolation.

   - **Examples**: Supportive friendships and close family bonds offer a sense of belonging and reassurance during challenging times, contributing to overall mental well-being.

2. **Stress Reduction and Coping**:

- **Overview**: Positive relationships can help manage stress and provide coping mechanisms for dealing with life's difficulties. Intimate connections offer a safe space to express concerns and seek advice, which can alleviate stress and improve mental health.

- **Examples**: Talking through problems with a trusted partner or friend can help alleviate anxiety, while physical affection and comforting gestures can reduce stress levels and promote relaxation.

3. **Self-Esteem and Self-Worth**:
   - **Overview**: Intimacy can positively impact self-esteem and self-worth by providing validation and affirmation. Feeling valued and understood in relationships can boost confidence and foster a positive self-image.

   - **Examples**: Positive reinforcement from loved ones, such as praise and encouragement, can enhance self-esteem and contribute to a healthier self-perception.

4. **Emotional Regulation and Resilience**:
   - **Overview**: Intimate relationships can aid in emotional regulation by offering a supportive environment for managing emotions. This support helps individuals build resilience and develop healthy coping strategies for emotional challenges.

   - **Examples**: Having a reliable source of comfort and understanding can help individuals navigate emotional ups and downs more effectively and build resilience in the face of adversity.

## The Psychological Benefits of Intimate Relationships

1. **Enhanced Life Satisfaction**:
   - **Overview**: Positive intimate relationships contribute to overall life satisfaction by providing companionship, support, and a sense of purpose. Feeling connected and valued in relationships enhances overall happiness and fulfillment.
   - **Examples**: Engaging in meaningful activities with loved ones, celebrating achievements together, and sharing life experiences can enhance life satisfaction and contribute to a sense of well-being.

2. **Reduction in Mental Health Issues**:
   - **Overview**: Strong, supportive relationships are associated with a lower risk of mental health issues such as depression and anxiety. Intimate connections provide emotional support and a buffer against mental health challenges.
   - **Examples**: Having a trusted friend or partner to talk to can reduce the risk of developing mental health issues and provide a source of comfort during difficult times.

3. **Improved Cognitive Function**:
   - **Overview**: Positive social interactions and intimate relationships can support cognitive function and mental clarity. Engaging in stimulating conversations and shared activities can keep the mind active and engaged.

- ◦ **Examples**: Participating in meaningful discussions, learning new things together, and engaging in shared hobbies can enhance cognitive function and mental sharpness.

4. **Increased Sense of Belonging**:

- ◦ **Overview**: Intimacy fosters a sense of belonging and connection, which is essential for mental health. Feeling accepted and included in relationships contributes to a positive self-concept and emotional stability.

- ◦ **Examples**: Being part of a close-knit group or having a supportive network provides a sense of belonging and reduces feelings of loneliness and isolation.

## Nurturing Intimate Relationships for Mental Health

1. **Prioritize Quality Time**:

- ◦ **Overview**: Spending quality time with loved ones strengthens emotional bonds and enhances mental well-being. Engaging in meaningful activities and conversations fosters deeper connections and contributes to emotional resilience.

- ◦ **Tips**: Schedule regular time for shared activities, practice active listening, and focus on creating positive experiences together.

2. **Foster Open Communication**:

- ◦ **Overview**: Open and honest communication is essential for maintaining healthy, supportive relationships. Expressing emotions, sharing thoughts, and discussing concerns contribute to stronger connections and better mental health.

- **Tips**: Practice active listening, be empathetic and understanding, and address issues openly and constructively.

3. **Cultivate Empathy and Understanding**:
   - **Overview**: Empathy and understanding are crucial for building and maintaining intimate relationships. Being empathetic helps individuals connect on a deeper level and provides emotional support during challenging times.
   - **Tips**: Practice empathy by actively trying to understand others' perspectives, validating their feelings, and offering support and encouragement.

4. **Seek Professional Help if Needed**:
   - **Overview**: If mental health issues arise or relationship difficulties impact well-being, seeking professional help can be beneficial. Therapy and counseling can provide valuable support for improving mental health and relationship dynamics.
   - **Tips**: Consider individual or couples therapy for addressing mental health concerns or relationship challenges. Professional guidance can offer strategies for improving emotional resilience and strengthening connections.

## Addressing Relationship Challenges for Mental Health

1. **Managing Conflict Constructively**:
   - **Overview**: Conflict is a natural part of relationships, but how it is managed can impact mental health. Constructive conflict resolution fosters understanding and strengthens relationships, contributing

to better mental well-being.

- **Tips**: Approach conflicts with a problem-solving mindset, avoid blame and criticism, and focus on finding mutually agreeable solutions.

2. **Maintaining Boundaries**:
   - **Overview**: Healthy boundaries are essential for maintaining balanced relationships and protecting mental health. Setting and respecting boundaries ensures that relationships remain supportive and fulfilling.
   - **Tips**: Communicate your needs and limits clearly, respect others' boundaries, and seek to establish a balance between personal space and connection.

3. **Addressing Unresolved Issues**:
   - **Overview**: Unresolved issues or past traumas can impact mental health and relationship dynamics. Addressing these issues openly and seeking resolution is important for maintaining healthy, supportive relationships.
   - **Tips**: Engage in open discussions about unresolved issues, consider therapy or counseling for addressing past traumas, and work towards finding closure and resolution.

## Conclusion

Intimacy and mental health are deeply interconnected, with positive relationships playing a crucial role in emotional well-being. Intimate connections provide emotional support, enhance life satisfaction, and contribute to psychological resilience. By nurturing meaningful relationships, prioritizing open communication, and addressing challenges constructively, individuals can foster better mental health and build stronger, more fulfilling connections.

In the next chapter, we will explore the concept of emotional intelligence and its role in enhancing intimacy. We will discuss how self-awareness, empathy, and emotional regulation contribute to developing and maintaining meaningful relationships. Join us as we continue our exploration of the dimensions of intimacy and their impact on our lives.

# CHAPTER 20: REBUILDING INTIMACY AFTER CONFLICT

Conflicts are an inevitable part of any relationship, but they can also serve as opportunities for growth and deeper connection. Rebuilding intimacy after a conflict involves navigating the challenges of forgiveness, communication, and mutual understanding. This chapter provides strategies for repairing and strengthening relationships following disagreements, emphasizing the importance of addressing issues constructively and fostering renewed closeness.

**Understanding the Nature of Conflict**

1. **Conflict as a Natural Component of Relationships**:
    - **Overview**: Conflicts are a natural and unavoidable aspect of relationships, arising from differences in opinions, values, and needs. While conflicts can be challenging, they also provide opportunities for growth and deeper understanding.

    - **Examples**: Disagreements about finances, household responsibilities, or personal goals can lead to conflicts, but addressing these issues constructively can strengthen the relationship.

2. **The Impact of Conflict on Intimacy**:
    - **Overview**: Conflicts can temporarily disrupt intimacy by causing emotional distance and creating feelings of hurt or frustration. However, addressing conflicts effectively can lead to a deeper understanding and stronger bond.
    - **Examples**: A heated argument may result in emotional withdrawal, but working through the conflict can ultimately enhance intimacy by improving communication and resolving underlying issues.

**Strategies for Rebuilding Intimacy After Conflict**

1. **Acknowledge and Validate Feelings**:
    - **Overview**: Acknowledging and validating each other's feelings is essential for rebuilding intimacy after a conflict. Understanding and respecting each other's emotions can help repair the emotional rift and restore trust.
    - **Tips**: Listen actively to each other's perspectives, express empathy, and validate each other's feelings without dismissing or minimizing them.

2. **Practice Open and Honest Communication**:
    - **Overview**: Effective communication is crucial for resolving conflicts and rebuilding intimacy. Open and honest dialogue helps clarify misunderstandings, address grievances, and find common ground.
    - **Tips**: Use "I" statements to express your feelings without placing blame, avoid interrupting, and seek to understand the other person's viewpoint. Focus on finding

solutions rather than dwelling on the problem.

3. **Seek Forgiveness and Offer Apologies**:
   - **Overview**: Forgiveness is a key component of rebuilding intimacy. Offering a sincere apology and seeking forgiveness helps heal emotional wounds and restore trust.
   - **Tips**: Acknowledge your role in the conflict, express genuine remorse, and take responsibility for your actions. Be willing to forgive the other person and let go of resentment.

4. **Rebuild Trust Through Consistent Actions**:
   - **Overview**: Trust is essential for intimacy, and rebuilding it requires consistent actions and behavior. Demonstrating reliability, honesty, and commitment helps restore confidence and strengthen the relationship.
   - **Tips**: Follow through on promises, be transparent in your actions, and show commitment to resolving the underlying issues. Rebuilding trust takes time and requires ongoing effort.

5. **Engage in Shared Activities and Quality Time**:
   - **Overview**: Spending quality time together and engaging in shared activities helps reinforce the bond and rebuild intimacy. Positive experiences and interactions contribute to emotional connection and satisfaction.
   - **Tips**: Plan activities that you both enjoy, create new positive memories, and make time for regular, meaningful interactions. Focus on strengthening the relationship

through shared experiences.

6. **Reflect on and Learn from the Conflict**:
   - **Overview**: Reflecting on the conflict and understanding its causes can provide valuable insights for future interactions. Learning from the experience helps prevent similar issues and fosters personal and relational growth.
   - **Tips**: Discuss what triggered the conflict, identify patterns or triggers, and explore ways to handle similar situations more effectively in the future. Use the insights gained to improve communication and understanding.

7. **Seek Professional Help if Needed**:
   - **Overview**: If conflicts persist or if rebuilding intimacy proves challenging, seeking professional help can provide valuable support. Therapy and counseling can offer strategies for resolving conflicts and enhancing relationships.
   - **Tips**: Consider couples therapy or individual counseling to address unresolved issues, improve communication skills, and strengthen the relationship. Professional guidance can offer new perspectives and tools for rebuilding intimacy.

## Preventing Future Conflicts

1. **Establish Healthy Communication Habits**:
   - **Overview**: Developing and maintaining healthy communication habits helps prevent conflicts and promotes a positive relationship dynamic. Open, respectful communication fosters understanding and

reduces misunderstandings.

- **Tips**: Practice active listening, express needs and concerns constructively, and address issues promptly. Regularly check in with each other to ensure mutual understanding and satisfaction.

2. **Set and Respect Boundaries**:
   - **Overview**: Establishing and respecting boundaries helps maintain a balanced relationship and prevents conflicts from arising. Clear boundaries contribute to mutual respect and understanding.
   - **Tips**: Communicate your boundaries clearly, respect your partner's boundaries, and address any concerns or discomfort promptly. Boundaries help define individual needs and prevent encroachment on personal space.

3. **Foster Emotional Resilience**:
   - **Overview**: Building emotional resilience helps individuals handle conflicts and challenges more effectively. Resilient individuals are better equipped to navigate difficult situations and maintain intimacy.
   - **Tips**: Practice self-care, develop coping strategies, and seek support when needed. Resilience contributes to emotional well-being and helps sustain healthy relationships.

4. **Cultivate a Positive Relationship Culture**:
   - **Overview**: Creating a positive relationship culture involves fostering mutual respect, appreciation, and support. A positive culture helps prevent conflicts and

strengthens the overall relationship dynamic.

- ◦ **Tips**: Express appreciation regularly, celebrate each other's successes, and support each other's goals. A positive relationship culture contributes to long-term satisfaction and intimacy.

## Conclusion

Rebuilding intimacy after a conflict requires effort, understanding, and commitment. By acknowledging feelings, practicing open communication, seeking forgiveness, and rebuilding trust, individuals can repair and strengthen their relationships. Engaging in shared activities, reflecting on conflicts, and seeking professional help when needed contribute to a healthier, more resilient relationship. Preventing future conflicts through healthy communication, boundaries, emotional resilience, and a positive relationship culture further supports the growth and depth of intimacy.

In the next chapter, we will explore the role of personal growth in enhancing intimacy. We will discuss how individual development, self-awareness, and personal fulfillment contribute to building and sustaining meaningful relationships. Join us as we continue our journey through the dimensions of intimacy and their impact on our lives.

# CHAPTER 21: INTIMACY IN PARENTHOOD

Parenthood is a transformative experience that introduces new dynamics into relationships. The arrival of a child brings joy and fulfillment but also brings new challenges that can impact intimacy between partners. This chapter explores how becoming parents affects intimacy, offering practical tips for maintaining a strong connection amidst the demands and changes of parenting.

**The Impact of Parenthood on Intimacy**

1. **Shifts in Priorities**:
   - **Overview**: Parenthood often shifts priorities as parents focus on the needs of their child. This shift can lead to changes in the time and attention given to the relationship, impacting intimacy.

   - **Examples**: Late-night feedings, sleep deprivation, and balancing work and parenting responsibilities can reduce the time available for couples to connect and nurture their relationship.

2. **Increased Stress and Fatigue**:
   - **Overview**: The demands of parenting can lead to increased stress and fatigue, affecting mood and interaction with

a partner. Stress can create emotional distance and reduce the quality of intimate connections.

- **Examples**: Managing a child's needs, dealing with sleepless nights, and navigating new responsibilities can lead to exhaustion and irritability, impacting relationship dynamics.

3. **Changing Relationship Dynamics**:
   - **Overview**: Parenthood often changes the dynamics of a relationship, including shifts in roles and responsibilities. These changes can affect how partners relate to each other and their sense of intimacy.

   - **Examples**: One partner may take on more childcare duties, leading to shifts in the balance of responsibilities and potentially causing feelings of imbalance or resentment.

**Strategies for Maintaining Intimacy in Parenthood**

1. **Prioritize Quality Time Together**:
   - **Overview**: Even with the demands of parenting, it is important to prioritize quality time together. Scheduling regular moments for connection helps maintain intimacy and reinforces the partnership.

   - **Tips**: Plan regular date nights, engage in activities you both enjoy, and create opportunities for meaningful conversations. Focus on spending intentional time together, even if it's brief.

2. **Communicate Openly and Honestly**:
   - **Overview**: Open and honest

communication is crucial for maintaining intimacy amidst the challenges of parenthood. Sharing feelings, concerns, and expectations helps manage stress and strengthens the relationship.

- **Tips**: Discuss parenting challenges, express appreciation, and address any concerns or frustrations openly. Regularly check in with each other about your needs and experiences.

3. **Support Each Other's Needs**:
   - **Overview**: Supporting each other's emotional and physical needs is essential for maintaining intimacy. Recognize and validate each other's experiences and offer support in managing the demands of parenting.
   - **Tips**: Offer help with childcare duties, share responsibilities, and provide encouragement and understanding. Acknowledge each other's efforts and offer assistance when needed.

4. **Foster Emotional Connection**:
   - **Overview**: Nurturing emotional connection helps maintain intimacy and reinforces the bond between partners. Emotional closeness is essential for a strong and supportive relationship.
   - **Tips**: Practice active listening, show empathy, and express affection and appreciation. Engage in meaningful conversations and share your feelings and experiences with each other.

5. **Maintain Physical Affection**:

- **Overview**: Physical affection is an important aspect of intimacy that should be maintained despite the demands of parenting. Small gestures of affection can reinforce the connection and strengthen the relationship.

- **Tips**: Make time for hugs, kisses, and physical closeness. Prioritize intimacy in daily routines and make an effort to connect physically, even amidst busy schedules.

6. **Set Boundaries and Create Space**:

   - **Overview**: Setting boundaries and creating space for each other is important for maintaining intimacy. Establishing boundaries helps balance personal time with parenting responsibilities.

   - **Tips**: Discuss and agree on boundaries regarding personal time and space. Ensure that both partners have opportunities to recharge and maintain individual interests.

7. **Seek Support and Resources**:

   - **Overview**: Seeking support and utilizing resources can help manage the challenges of parenthood and maintain intimacy. Support from family, friends, or professionals can provide valuable assistance.

   - **Tips**: Reach out to support networks, consider parenting classes or counseling, and seek advice from trusted sources. Utilize available resources to manage parenting challenges and strengthen the relationship.

**Navigating Common Challenges**

1. **Dealing with Sleep Deprivation**:

- **Overview**: Sleep deprivation is a common challenge for new parents and can affect mood and intimacy. Managing sleep-related issues is important for maintaining emotional well-being and connection.

- **Tips**: Develop a sleep plan, share nighttime duties, and prioritize rest whenever possible. Communicate about sleep-related challenges and work together to find solutions.

2. **Balancing Work and Parenting**:
   - **Overview**: Balancing work and parenting responsibilities can be challenging and may impact time spent together. Finding a balance is crucial for maintaining intimacy and managing stress.

   - **Tips**: Establish a routine that accommodates work and parenting responsibilities, set clear boundaries between work and home life, and prioritize family time.

3. **Managing Differences in Parenting Styles**:
   - **Overview**: Differences in parenting styles can lead to conflicts and affect intimacy. Addressing these differences constructively is important for maintaining a harmonious relationship.

   - **Tips**: Discuss and align on parenting approaches, respect each other's perspectives, and work towards common goals. Seek compromise and find ways to support each other's parenting styles.

4. **Handling Relationship Strain**:
   - **Overview**: Parenthood can strain

relationships and lead to feelings of frustration or disconnection. Addressing relationship strain proactively helps maintain intimacy and strengthen the bond.

- **Tips**: Address issues openly, seek professional help if needed, and prioritize relationship maintenance. Focus on problem-solving and nurturing the connection amidst challenges.

## Conclusion

Parenthood introduces new dynamics into relationships, but with intentional effort and effective strategies, intimacy can be maintained and strengthened. Prioritizing quality time, practicing open communication, supporting each other, and managing challenges constructively are key to preserving intimacy amidst the demands of parenting. By nurturing the emotional and physical connection, partners can navigate the challenges of parenthood while deepening their bond and fostering a fulfilling relationship.

In the next chapter, we will explore the concept of intimacy in personal growth and self-development. We will discuss how individual growth and self-awareness contribute to building and sustaining meaningful relationships. Join us as we continue our exploration of intimacy and its impact on our lives.

# CHAPTER 22: INTIMACY IN LATER LIFE

As people age, the nature of their relationships and the ways they experience intimacy evolve. Intimacy remains a crucial aspect of relationships in later life, bringing both unique challenges and opportunities. This chapter explores how intimacy manifests in later life, providing insights into maintaining and nurturing intimate connections as individuals navigate the aging process.

**Understanding Intimacy in Later Life**

1. **Evolving Relationship Dynamics**:
   - **Overview**: Relationships in later life often experience shifts in dynamics due to changing life circumstances, such as retirement, health issues, or the loss of loved ones. These changes can impact how intimacy is experienced and expressed.
   - **Examples**: Retiring from work can alter daily routines and interactions, while dealing with health issues may affect physical closeness and emotional connection.

2. **The Role of Longevity and Life Experience**:
   - **Overview**: Longevity and accumulated life experiences influence how intimacy

is understood and valued in later life. Long-term relationships may reflect deep emotional bonds, while new relationships may bring fresh perspectives on intimacy.

- **Examples**: Older adults in long-term marriages may experience intimacy through shared history and understanding, while new relationships may offer opportunities for renewed connection and exploration.

3. **Challenges of Aging**:
   - **Overview**: Aging presents challenges that can impact intimacy, including health problems, mobility issues, and the loss of partners or friends. Addressing these challenges is important for maintaining intimate connections.

   - **Examples**: Physical limitations or chronic illnesses may affect the ability to engage in traditional expressions of intimacy, requiring adaptations and new ways of connecting.

**Strategies for Maintaining Intimacy in Later Life**

1. **Emphasize Emotional Connection**:
   - **Overview**: Emotional connection remains a cornerstone of intimacy in later life. Fostering emotional closeness involves maintaining open communication, sharing feelings, and providing support.

   - **Tips**: Engage in meaningful conversations, express appreciation and affection, and offer emotional support. Focus on building a deep understanding and connection through shared experiences.

2. **Adapt Physical Intimacy**:
     - **Overview**: Physical intimacy may need to adapt due to age-related changes, but it remains an important aspect of relationships. Finding new ways to express physical closeness can help maintain intimacy.
     - **Tips**: Explore different forms of physical affection, such as holding hands, gentle touch, or cuddling. Adjust physical expressions of intimacy to accommodate any health or mobility issues.

3. **Maintain Shared Activities and Interests**:
     - **Overview**: Continuing to engage in shared activities and interests strengthens the bond between partners. Finding activities that both individuals enjoy can enhance intimacy and provide opportunities for connection.
     - **Tips**: Participate in hobbies, attend events, or take up new interests together. Shared experiences contribute to emotional closeness and offer positive interactions.

4. **Foster Mutual Support**:
     - **Overview**: Providing and receiving support is crucial for maintaining intimacy in later life. Mutual support helps partners navigate challenges and reinforces the sense of partnership and connection.
     - **Tips**: Offer assistance with daily tasks, provide emotional encouragement, and be attentive to each other's needs. Mutual support strengthens the bond and helps manage the challenges of aging.

5. **Explore New Ways to Connect**:
    - **Overview**: As life circumstances change, exploring new ways to connect can help maintain intimacy. Being open to new experiences and adjustments allows for continued growth in the relationship.
    - **Tips**: Embrace technology for communication, try new activities or experiences together, and adapt relationship practices to fit current needs. Flexibility and creativity contribute to sustaining intimacy.

6. **Address Loneliness and Social Isolation**:
    - **Overview**: Loneliness and social isolation can affect intimacy, especially if social networks shrink with age. Addressing these issues is important for maintaining emotional well-being and connection.
    - **Tips**: Stay connected with family and friends, join social groups or clubs, and engage in community activities. Building and maintaining social connections supports intimacy and overall well-being.

7. **Celebrate Relationship Milestones**:
    - **Overview**: Celebrating relationship milestones and achievements reinforces the bond and acknowledges the importance of the relationship. Milestones provide opportunities to reflect on and appreciate the journey together.
    - **Tips**: Commemorate anniversaries, significant events, and achievements. Reflect on shared experiences and express gratitude for the journey and the

relationship.

## Navigating Common Challenges

1. **Dealing with Health Issues**:
   - **Overview**: Health issues can impact intimacy by affecting physical abilities and emotional well-being. Addressing health-related challenges with sensitivity and support helps maintain intimacy.
   - **Tips**: Communicate openly about health concerns, adjust activities and physical intimacy as needed, and provide emotional support. Seek medical assistance and resources to manage health challenges together.

2. **Managing Grief and Loss**:
   - **Overview**: Grief and loss, such as the death of a partner or close friends, can impact intimacy and emotional connection. Navigating grief requires sensitivity and mutual support.
   - **Tips**: Allow time for grieving, offer comfort and understanding, and seek support from counseling or support groups. Acknowledge the impact of loss and work together to heal and maintain the connection.

3. **Maintaining Independence and Autonomy**:
   - **Overview**: Balancing independence and intimacy is important as individuals age. Respecting each other's need for autonomy while nurturing the relationship helps maintain a healthy dynamic.
   - **Tips**: Support each other's interests and independence, communicate about personal

needs, and find a balance between personal space and togetherness. Respecting autonomy fosters mutual respect and intimacy.

4. **Addressing Financial Concerns**:
    - **Overview**: Financial concerns can affect relationships and intimacy, especially in later life. Addressing financial issues with transparency and collaboration helps manage stress and maintain connection.

    - **Tips**: Discuss financial matters openly, work together on budgeting and planning, and seek financial advice if needed. Financial stability and communication contribute to relationship health.

## Conclusion

Intimacy remains a vital aspect of relationships throughout later life, despite the unique challenges and changes that come with aging. By emphasizing emotional connection, adapting physical intimacy, engaging in shared activities, and providing mutual support, individuals can maintain and strengthen their relationships as they navigate the aging process. Addressing common challenges with sensitivity and collaboration fosters resilience and deepens the bond.

In the next chapter, we will explore the concept of intimacy in the context of self-growth and personal development. We will discuss how personal growth and self-awareness contribute to building and sustaining meaningful relationships. Join us as we continue our exploration of intimacy and its impact on our lives.

# CHAPTER 23: INTIMACY AND SELF-DISCOVERY

Understanding oneself is foundational to developing and nurturing intimate relationships with others. Self-discovery involves exploring and understanding one's identity, values, emotions, and desires. This chapter delves into the journey of self-discovery, examining its impact on intimacy and offering insights into how personal growth can enhance relational connections.

**The Journey of Self-Discovery**

1. **Understanding Self-Discovery**:
    - **Overview**: Self-discovery is the process of exploring and understanding one's inner self, including thoughts, feelings, values, and aspirations. This journey is essential for personal growth and plays a critical role in building meaningful relationships.

    - **Components**: Self-awareness, self-acceptance, and personal reflection are key components of self-discovery. These aspects help individuals understand their needs and boundaries, leading to healthier and more fulfilling relationships.

2. **The Role of Self-Awareness**:
    - **Overview**: Self-awareness involves

recognizing and understanding one's emotions, motivations, and behaviors. It is crucial for developing intimacy, as it enables individuals to communicate effectively and connect more deeply with others.

- **Examples**: Understanding personal triggers, emotional responses, and core values helps individuals interact more authentically and empathetically in relationships.

3. **The Importance of Self-Acceptance**:
    - **Overview**: Self-acceptance involves embracing one's strengths and weaknesses without judgment. It fosters confidence and authenticity, which are essential for forming genuine connections with others.

    - **Examples**: Accepting one's imperfections and being comfortable with one's identity allows individuals to engage in relationships with greater openness and vulnerability.

4. **The Impact of Personal Reflection**:
    - **Overview**: Personal reflection involves contemplating one's experiences, choices, and growth. Reflecting on past relationships and personal growth can provide valuable insights for enhancing intimacy in current and future relationships.

    - **Examples**: Reflecting on past relationship patterns and personal growth can help individuals identify areas for improvement and develop healthier relational dynamics.

**How Self-Discovery Enhances Intimacy**

1. **Improving Communication**:

- **Overview**: Self-discovery enhances communication by helping individuals express their needs, desires, and emotions more clearly and authentically. Effective communication is vital for building and maintaining intimacy.

- **Tips**: Share personal insights, express feelings openly, and be honest about needs and expectations. Clear and authentic communication fosters mutual understanding and connection.

2. **Building Emotional Intelligence**:

   - **Overview**: Emotional intelligence involves understanding and managing one's emotions and recognizing the emotions of others. Developing emotional intelligence through self-discovery enhances empathy and connection in relationships.

   - **Tips**: Practice active listening, validate others' feelings, and respond with empathy. Emotional intelligence helps navigate relational challenges and strengthen emotional bonds.

3. **Fostering Authenticity**:

   - **Overview**: Self-discovery promotes authenticity by encouraging individuals to embrace their true selves. Authenticity is crucial for developing deep and meaningful connections with others.

   - **Tips**: Be true to your values, express your genuine self, and avoid pretending to be someone you're not. Authentic interactions build trust and strengthen intimacy.

4. **Setting Healthy Boundaries**:

- **Overview**: Understanding oneself allows individuals to set and maintain healthy boundaries in relationships. Clear boundaries protect emotional well-being and contribute to balanced and respectful connections.

- **Tips**: Identify personal boundaries, communicate them clearly, and respect others' boundaries. Healthy boundaries create a foundation for mutual respect and intimacy.

5. **Enhancing Self-Esteem**:
   - **Overview**: Self-discovery contributes to self-esteem by fostering self-acceptance and personal growth. Healthy self-esteem supports positive relational dynamics and confidence in intimate connections.

   - **Tips**: Recognize and celebrate personal achievements, practice self-compassion, and engage in activities that build confidence. A positive self-image enhances relational interactions and intimacy.

6. **Navigating Relational Patterns**:
   - **Overview**: Reflecting on past relational patterns and experiences helps individuals understand how they interact with others. This awareness allows for growth and improvement in relational dynamics.

   - **Tips**: Analyze past relationship experiences, identify recurring patterns, and address any challenges or issues. Understanding and addressing relational patterns contribute to healthier and more fulfilling connections.

**Practical Steps for Self-Discovery**

1. **Engage in Self-Reflection**:
     - **Overview**: Regular self-reflection helps individuals gain insights into their thoughts, feelings, and behaviors. Engaging in reflective practices supports personal growth and enhances relational connections.
     - **Tips**: Keep a journal, meditate, or engage in introspective activities. Reflect on personal experiences, goals, and values to gain a deeper understanding of oneself.

2. **Seek Feedback and Support**:
     - **Overview**: Seeking feedback from trusted friends, family, or professionals can provide valuable perspectives on one's self-discovery journey. Support from others helps in understanding oneself and improving relational dynamics.
     - **Tips**: Ask for constructive feedback, participate in counseling or therapy, and engage in support groups. Utilize external perspectives to enhance self-awareness and growth.

3. **Set Personal Goals**:
     - **Overview**: Setting personal goals encourages growth and development, contributing to self-discovery and improved relational dynamics. Goals provide direction and motivation for personal and relational growth.
     - **Tips**: Identify areas for personal development, set achievable goals, and create a plan for reaching them. Regularly evaluate progress and adjust goals as

needed.

4. **Cultivate Mindfulness**:
    - **Overview**: Mindfulness involves being present and aware of one's thoughts, feelings, and experiences. Practicing mindfulness supports self-discovery and enhances emotional connection in relationships.

    - **Tips**: Practice mindfulness through meditation, deep breathing exercises, or mindful activities. Cultivating mindfulness helps manage emotions and improve relational interactions.

5. **Explore Personal Interests**:
    - **Overview**: Exploring personal interests and passions contributes to self-discovery and personal fulfillment. Engaging in activities that bring joy and satisfaction supports personal growth and enhances relationships.

    - **Tips**: Pursue hobbies, engage in creative projects, or try new activities. Personal interests enrich one's life and contribute to a well-rounded and fulfilling relationship.

## Conclusion

Self-discovery is a fundamental aspect of developing and nurturing intimate relationships. By understanding oneself, individuals can communicate more effectively, build emotional intelligence, and foster authenticity in their interactions. Personal growth through self-discovery enhances relational connections, contributing to deeper and more meaningful relationships.

In the next chapter, we will explore the role of intimacy in personal development and self-growth. We will discuss how self-awareness and personal growth contribute to building and sustaining meaningful connections with others. Join us as we continue our exploration of intimacy and its impact on our lives.

# CHAPTER 24: MINDFULNESS AND INTIMACY

Mindfulness, the practice of being fully present and engaged in the moment, offers profound benefits for enhancing intimacy in relationships. By fostering a deeper awareness of oneself and one's partner, mindfulness can transform relational dynamics, improve communication, and strengthen emotional bonds. This chapter explores the intersection of mindfulness and intimacy, highlighting its benefits and offering practical exercises for cultivating mindfulness in relationships.

**Understanding Mindfulness and Its Impact on Intimacy**

1. **Defining Mindfulness**:
   - **Overview**: Mindfulness is the practice of paying deliberate attention to the present moment without judgment. It involves being fully aware of thoughts, emotions, and sensations as they arise.

   - **Components**: Key components of mindfulness include awareness, acceptance, and presence. These elements contribute to a deeper understanding of oneself and one's partner, enhancing relational connection.

2. **The Connection Between Mindfulness and Intimacy**:

- **Overview**: Mindfulness enhances intimacy by promoting awareness, empathy, and presence in relationships. It enables individuals to connect more deeply with their partners and respond more effectively to relational needs.

- **Examples**: Mindful listening allows partners to truly hear and understand each other's perspectives, while mindful presence fosters a deeper emotional connection.

**Benefits of Mindfulness for Intimacy**

1. **Improved Communication**:
   - **Overview**: Mindfulness improves communication by encouraging active listening and thoughtful responses. Being present in conversations allows individuals to engage more fully and respond with greater empathy.

   - **Examples**: Mindful listening involves focusing entirely on the speaker without interrupting or formulating a response prematurely. This approach fosters mutual understanding and respect.

2. **Enhanced Emotional Connection**:
   - **Overview**: Mindfulness deepens emotional connections by promoting awareness of one's own emotions and those of one's partner. This heightened awareness fosters empathy and emotional intimacy.

   - **Examples**: Mindful awareness of emotions allows individuals to express feelings more authentically and respond more empathetically to their partner's emotions.

3. **Reduced Reactivity and Conflict**:
   - **Overview**: Mindfulness helps manage emotional reactivity and reduces the likelihood of conflict. By cultivating a non-reactive stance, individuals can address issues more calmly and constructively.
   - **Examples**: Mindful breathing and awareness can help individuals pause and choose a thoughtful response rather than reacting impulsively during conflicts.

4. **Increased Presence and Attention**:
   - **Overview**: Mindfulness fosters a greater sense of presence and attention in relationships. Being fully engaged in the moment enhances the quality of interactions and strengthens relational bonds.
   - **Examples**: Mindful presence during shared activities, such as meals or conversations, enhances the sense of connection and mutual engagement.

5. **Strengthened Empathy and Understanding**:
   - **Overview**: Mindfulness enhances empathy by encouraging individuals to tune into their partner's experiences and emotions. This empathetic understanding fosters a deeper relational connection.
   - **Examples**: Mindful awareness of non-verbal cues and emotional states helps individuals respond with greater sensitivity and support.

**Practical Exercises for Cultivating Mindfulness in Relationships**

1. **Mindful Listening**:
    - **Overview**: Mindful listening involves giving full attention to the speaker, acknowledging their feelings, and responding thoughtfully. This practice enhances communication and connection.
    - **Exercise**:
        1. Choose a time for a conversation with your partner.
        2. Focus entirely on your partner's words, avoiding distractions.
        3. Reflect on their feelings and perspectives before responding.
        4. Validate their experience and offer a thoughtful response.

2. **Mindful Breathing**:
    - **Overview**: Mindful breathing helps individuals center themselves and manage stress. Practicing mindful breathing together can enhance relaxation and emotional connection.
    - **Exercise**:
        1. Sit comfortably with your partner.
        2. Close your eyes and take deep, slow breaths.
        3. Focus on the sensation of each breath and the rhythm of your breathing.
        4. Encourage each other to stay present and relaxed.

3. **Mindful Appreciation**:
    - **Overview**: Mindful appreciation involves consciously acknowledging and expressing

gratitude for your partner's positive qualities and actions. This practice fosters a sense of connection and appreciation.

- **Exercise**:
    1. Take a moment each day to reflect on something you appreciate about your partner.
    2. Share your appreciation with them, focusing on specific qualities or actions.
    3. Practice gratitude regularly to reinforce positive feelings and connection.

4. **Mindful Touch**:
   - **Overview**: Mindful touch involves being fully present and aware during physical interactions. This practice enhances the quality of physical intimacy and connection.
   - **Exercise**:
       1. Choose a moment for physical touch, such as a hug or holding hands.
       2. Focus on the sensations and feelings associated with the touch.
       3. Be attentive to your partner's responses and adjust your touch accordingly.
       4. Practice mindful touch regularly to deepen physical and emotional connection.

5. **Mindful Reflection**:
   - **Overview**: Mindful reflection involves taking time to reflect on relational

experiences and personal growth. This practice helps individuals gain insights and improve relational dynamics.

- **Exercise**:
  1. Set aside time for reflection, individually or with your partner.
  2. Consider recent interactions, emotions, and experiences.
  3. Discuss insights and observations with your partner, focusing on growth and improvement.
  4. Use reflection to identify areas for development and celebrate positive changes.

6. **Mindful Conflict Resolution**:
   - **Overview**: Mindful conflict resolution involves addressing disagreements with awareness and empathy. This approach promotes constructive dialogue and effective problem-solving.
   - **Exercise**:
     1. When a conflict arises, take a moment to pause and breathe.
     2. Focus on understanding your partner's perspective and emotions.
     3. Communicate openly and respectfully, using "I" statements to express your feelings.
     4. Work together to find a resolution that respects both perspectives.

## Overcoming Challenges in Mindful Practice

1. **Managing Distractions**:

- **Overview**: Distractions can hinder mindfulness practice. Identifying and managing distractions helps maintain focus and presence in relationships.
- **Tips**: Create a distraction-free environment for mindfulness exercises, and gently redirect your attention when distractions arise.

2. **Cultivating Consistency**:
   - **Overview**: Consistency is key to developing mindfulness habits. Regular practice enhances the benefits and supports relational growth.
   - **Tips**: Incorporate mindfulness practices into daily routines, set reminders, and commit to regular practice.

3. **Addressing Resistance**:
   - **Overview**: Resistance to mindfulness practice may arise due to discomfort or skepticism. Addressing resistance with openness and patience supports ongoing practice.
   - **Tips**: Approach mindfulness with curiosity and non-judgment. Be patient with yourself and your partner as you develop mindfulness skills.

## Conclusion

Mindfulness offers significant benefits for enhancing intimacy in relationships by promoting awareness, empathy, and presence. By engaging in mindful practices such as mindful listening, breathing, and appreciation, individuals can deepen their emotional connections and improve relational dynamics. Cultivating mindfulness fosters a more authentic and supportive relationship, enriching the quality of intimate connections.

In the next chapter, we will explore the role of self-compassion in building and maintaining intimate relationships. We will discuss how self-compassion contributes to personal growth and relational health, offering practical strategies for integrating self-compassion into daily interactions. Join us as we continue our journey through the exploration of intimacy and its impact on our lives.

# CHAPTER 25: THE SCIENCE OF INTIMACY

Intimacy, a crucial component of human relationships, has been the subject of extensive scientific research. Understanding the nature and effects of intimacy from a psychological and physiological perspective provides valuable insights into how intimate connections influence our lives. This chapter explores key findings from scientific studies, highlighting the mechanisms and benefits of intimacy.

**Psychological Perspectives on Intimacy**

1. **Attachment Theory**:
   - **Overview**: Attachment theory, developed by John Bowlby, suggests that early relationships with caregivers shape our patterns of intimacy in adult relationships. Secure attachment fosters healthy intimacy, while insecure attachment can lead to relational challenges.

   - **Key Findings**: Research indicates that individuals with secure attachment styles are more likely to experience satisfying and stable intimate relationships. In contrast, those with anxious or avoidant attachment styles may struggle with intimacy due to fear of rejection or closeness.

2. **The Role of Emotional Intelligence**:
   - **Overview**: Emotional intelligence (EI) involves the ability to understand, manage, and express emotions effectively. High EI is associated with better relationship quality and deeper intimacy.
   - **Key Findings**: Studies show that individuals with high EI are better at communicating, empathizing, and resolving conflicts, all of which enhance intimacy. Emotional intelligence training can improve relational skills and foster closer connections.

3. **Interpersonal Communication**:
   - **Overview**: Effective communication is critical for developing and maintaining intimacy. Research on interpersonal communication highlights the importance of active listening, self-disclosure, and empathy.
   - **Key Findings**: Couples who engage in open and honest communication report higher levels of intimacy and relationship satisfaction. Skills such as active listening and expressing appreciation are linked to stronger emotional bonds.

4. **Self-Disclosure and Intimacy**:
   - **Overview**: Self-disclosure, the act of revealing personal thoughts and feelings, is a fundamental aspect of building intimacy. Gradual and reciprocal self-disclosure fosters trust and emotional closeness.
   - **Key Findings**: Research suggests that appropriate self-disclosure enhances intimacy by creating a sense of mutual

understanding and vulnerability. Excessive or premature self-disclosure, however, can overwhelm or alienate partners.

5. **The Importance of Trust**:
    - **Overview**: Trust is a cornerstone of intimate relationships. Trusting relationships are characterized by honesty, reliability, and emotional safety.
    - **Key Findings**: Studies indicate that trust is positively correlated with relationship satisfaction and stability. Building and maintaining trust involves consistent behavior, open communication, and mutual respect.

**Physiological Perspectives on Intimacy**

1. **Oxytocin and Bonding**:
    - **Overview**: Oxytocin, often referred to as the "love hormone," plays a significant role in bonding and intimacy. It is released during physical touch, sexual activity, and emotional connection.
    - **Key Findings**: Research shows that oxytocin promotes feelings of trust, attachment, and emotional closeness. Higher levels of oxytocin are associated with greater relationship satisfaction and stability.

2. **The Stress-Reducing Effects of Intimacy**:
    - **Overview**: Intimate relationships have been shown to reduce stress and promote overall well-being. Physical touch and emotional support trigger physiological responses that alleviate stress.
    - **Key Findings**: Studies demonstrate that

intimate interactions, such as hugging or holding hands, lower cortisol levels (a stress hormone) and increase feelings of calm and security. Supportive relationships are linked to better mental and physical health.

3. **The Impact of Sexual Intimacy**:
    - **Overview**: Sexual intimacy contributes to emotional bonding and relationship satisfaction. It also has physiological benefits, including stress relief and improved mood.

    - **Key Findings**: Research indicates that regular sexual activity releases endorphins and oxytocin, enhancing emotional connection and reducing stress. Sexual satisfaction is positively correlated with overall relationship satisfaction.

4. **The Role of Non-Sexual Physical Touch**:
    - **Overview**: Non-sexual physical touch, such as hugging, cuddling, and holding hands, plays a crucial role in maintaining intimacy. Touch communicates affection, support, and reassurance.

    - **Key Findings**: Studies reveal that non-sexual touch increases oxytocin levels, reduces stress, and enhances emotional connection. Couples who engage in frequent physical touch report higher levels of intimacy and relationship satisfaction.

5. **The Influence of Hormonal Changes**:
    - **Overview**: Hormonal changes throughout life can impact intimacy and sexual desire. Understanding these changes can help couples navigate challenges and maintain

intimacy.

- ○ **Key Findings**: Research on hormonal changes, such as those occurring during menopause or andropause, highlights their effects on intimacy. Open communication and mutual support can help couples adapt to these changes and maintain a strong connection.

**Integrating Psychological and Physiological Insights**

1. **Holistic Understanding of Intimacy**:
   - ○ **Overview**: Integrating psychological and physiological perspectives provides a comprehensive understanding of intimacy. Both dimensions interact to shape relational dynamics and well-being.
   - ○ **Examples**: Emotional intelligence enhances communication, while oxytocin strengthens bonding. Effective communication reduces stress, while physical touch boosts emotional connection.

2. **Applying Research Findings to Relationships**:
   - ○ **Overview**: Applying insights from research can enhance intimacy in relationships. Understanding the science of intimacy empowers individuals to cultivate deeper connections.
   - ○ **Tips**: Practice emotional intelligence, engage in regular physical touch, communicate openly, and build trust. Integrating these practices fosters a holistic approach to intimacy.

3. **The Importance of Ongoing Learning and Growth**:

- ○ **Overview**: Intimacy is a dynamic process that evolves over time. Continued learning and personal growth are essential for sustaining intimate relationships.

- ○ **Tips**: Stay informed about the latest research on intimacy, seek personal development opportunities, and prioritize relational growth. Embrace change and adapt to evolving relational needs.

## Conclusion

The science of intimacy reveals fascinating insights into the psychological and physiological mechanisms that underpin close relationships. By understanding the role of attachment, emotional intelligence, communication, trust, and physiological processes, individuals can enhance their relational dynamics and foster deeper connections. Integrating these scientific findings into daily life promotes healthier, more satisfying intimate relationships.

In the next chapter, we will explore the role of self-compassion in building and maintaining intimate relationships. We will discuss how self-compassion contributes to personal growth and relational health, offering practical strategies for integrating self-compassion into daily interactions. Join us as we continue our journey through the exploration of intimacy and its impact on our lives.

# CHAPTER 26: INTIMACY IN LGBTQ + RELATIONSHIPS

Intimacy in LGBTQ+ relationships encompasses unique dynamics and challenges that often differ from those in heterosexual relationships. This chapter explores the experiences of LGBTQ+ individuals in intimate relationships, emphasizing the importance of acceptance, understanding, and support. By recognizing and addressing these unique aspects, we can foster deeper connections and promote healthy, fulfilling relationships for LGBTQ+ individuals.

**Understanding Intimacy in LGBTQ+ Relationships**

1. **Unique Challenges:**
   - **Overview**: LGBTQ+ relationships often face distinct challenges, including societal prejudice, discrimination, and internalized homophobia or transphobia. These challenges can impact intimacy and relationship dynamics.

   - **Examples**: Couples may encounter rejection from family or friends, experience social stigma, or face legal and institutional barriers that can strain their relationship.

2. **Diverse Identities and Experiences:**
   - **Overview**: LGBTQ+ relationships are diverse, encompassing a wide range of

identities and experiences. Understanding this diversity is crucial for fostering acceptance and intimacy.

- ○ **Examples**: Relationships may involve individuals who identify as gay, lesbian, bisexual, transgender, non-binary, or queer, each bringing unique perspectives and experiences to the relationship.

3. **Intersectionality**:

- ○ **Overview**: Intersectionality refers to the interconnected nature of social identities, such as race, gender, sexuality, and class, and how these intersections impact experiences of intimacy.

- ○ **Examples**: An LGBTQ+ individual who is also a person of color may face compounded challenges related to both racial and sexual identity, influencing their intimate relationships.

## The Role of Acceptance and Understanding

1. **Self-Acceptance and Authenticity**:

- ○ **Overview**: Self-acceptance is fundamental for developing authentic and intimate relationships. Embracing one's identity fosters confidence and openness in relationships.

- ○ **Key Points**: Encourage self-exploration and acceptance, celebrate individuality, and reject societal pressures to conform to heteronormative standards.

2. **Partner Acceptance**:

- ○ **Overview**: Acceptance from one's partner is crucial for intimacy. A supportive and understanding partner creates a safe space for vulnerability and emotional connection.

- **Key Points**: Practice active listening, validate your partner's experiences, and affirm their identity. Acceptance fosters trust and deepens emotional bonds.

3. **Social Support and Community**:
- **Overview**: Support from friends, family, and the broader LGBTQ+ community enhances relationship resilience and intimacy. A strong support network provides validation and understanding.
- **Key Points**: Seek out LGBTQ+ support groups, engage in community activities, and build connections with supportive individuals and organizations.

**Intimacy and Communication in LGBTQ+ Relationships**

1. **Open Communication**:
- **Overview**: Effective communication is essential for navigating the unique challenges of LGBTQ+ relationships. Open dialogue promotes understanding and connection.
- **Key Points**: Discuss identity, boundaries, and experiences openly. Address any issues related to societal prejudice or discrimination together.

2. **Navigating Disclosure**:
- **Overview**: Disclosure, or "coming out," is a significant aspect of LGBTQ+ relationships. Deciding when and how to disclose one's identity to others can impact intimacy.
- **Key Points**: Support each other in the

coming-out process, respect individual timelines, and discuss strategies for dealing with potential reactions from others.

3. **Managing Minority Stress**:
   - **Overview**: Minority stress refers to the unique stressors experienced by LGBTQ+ individuals due to societal prejudice and discrimination. Managing this stress is crucial for intimacy.
   - **Key Points**: Develop coping strategies, seek mental health support if needed, and engage in stress-reducing activities together.

## Physical and Sexual Intimacy in LGBTQ+ Relationships

1. **Exploring Physical Intimacy**:
   - **Overview**: Physical intimacy, including non-sexual touch and affection, is vital for connection. Understanding and respecting each other's needs enhances intimacy.
   - **Key Points**: Communicate openly about comfort levels, preferences, and boundaries. Engage in activities that promote physical closeness, such as cuddling or holding hands.

2. **Sexual Intimacy and Pleasure**:
   - **Overview**: Sexual intimacy is an important aspect of many LGBTQ+ relationships. Exploring and understanding each other's desires and boundaries fosters a fulfilling sexual connection.
   - **Key Points**: Discuss sexual desires, boundaries, and any concerns openly. Prioritize consent and mutual pleasure, and consider seeking resources or education on

LGBTQ+ sexual health.

3. **Addressing Sexual Health**:
    - **Overview**: Sexual health is crucial for maintaining intimacy. Understanding and addressing specific health needs related to LGBTQ+ individuals promotes a healthy and satisfying relationship.

    - **Key Points**: Educate yourselves about LGBTQ+ sexual health, practice safe sex, and seek regular health check-ups. Address any health concerns together.

## Strategies for Fostering Intimacy in LGBTQ+ Relationships

1. **Building Trust and Security**:
    - **Overview**: Trust and security are fundamental for intimacy. Creating a safe and supportive environment allows for vulnerability and deep connection.

    - **Key Points**: Be reliable, communicate openly, and support each other through challenges. Trust-building activities, such as shared hobbies or experiences, can strengthen bonds.

2. **Cultivating Empathy and Understanding**:
    - **Overview**: Empathy involves understanding and sharing your partner's feelings and experiences. Cultivating empathy enhances emotional intimacy.

    - **Key Points**: Practice active listening, validate your partner's emotions, and strive to understand their perspective. Empathy deepens emotional connection and support.

3. **Engaging in Shared Activities**:
    - **Overview**: Shared activities and interests

foster connection and intimacy. Engaging in activities that both partners enjoy strengthens relational bonds.

- **Key Points**: Plan regular activities together, explore new hobbies, and prioritize quality time. Shared experiences create lasting memories and deepen connection.

4. **Seeking Professional Support**:
   - **Overview**: Professional support, such as therapy or counseling, can be beneficial for addressing challenges and enhancing intimacy in LGBTQ+ relationships.
   - **Key Points**: Consider seeking LGBTQ + affirmative therapy or counseling to navigate relational challenges, improve communication, and build intimacy.

## Conclusion

Intimacy in LGBTQ+ relationships involves navigating unique challenges and dynamics. By fostering acceptance, understanding, and open communication, LGBTQ+ individuals can build deep, fulfilling connections. Recognizing and addressing the specific needs and experiences of LGBTQ + partners enhances intimacy and promotes relational resilience.

In the next chapter, we will explore the role of self-compassion in building and maintaining intimate relationships. We will discuss how self-compassion contributes to personal growth and relational health, offering practical strategies for integrating self-compassion into daily interactions. Join us as we continue our journey through the exploration of intimacy and its impact on our lives.

# CHAPTER 27: OVERCOMING INTIMACY ISSUES

Intimacy is a fundamental aspect of human relationships, yet many people encounter challenges in developing and maintaining it. These issues can arise from various sources, including past experiences, personal insecurities, and relational dynamics. This chapter identifies common intimacy issues and provides strategies for addressing them, focusing on communication, empathy, and self-awareness.

**Common Intimacy Issues**

1. **Fear of Vulnerability**:
   - **Overview**: Fear of vulnerability can prevent individuals from opening up and forming deep connections. This fear often stems from past hurts or rejection.

   - **Key Points**: Vulnerability is essential for intimacy, but it requires courage and trust. Understanding the sources of this fear can help in overcoming it.

2. **Insecurity and Low Self-Esteem**:
   - **Overview**: Insecurity and low self-esteem can lead to doubts about one's worthiness of love and affection, hindering intimacy.

   - **Key Points**: Building self-esteem and self-acceptance is crucial for developing healthy intimate relationships.

3. **Past Trauma**:
   - **Overview**: Traumatic experiences, such as abuse or betrayal, can create barriers to intimacy by causing fear, distrust, and emotional withdrawal.
   - **Key Points**: Healing from trauma is a complex process that often requires professional support and self-compassion.

4. **Communication Issues**:
   - **Overview**: Poor communication can lead to misunderstandings, conflicts, and emotional distance, all of which undermine intimacy.
   - **Key Points**: Effective communication is essential for expressing needs, resolving conflicts, and building emotional connection.

5. **Emotional Unavailability**:
   - **Overview**: Emotional unavailability, whether due to personal issues or relational dynamics, can prevent the development of deep connections.
   - **Key Points**: Recognizing and addressing emotional unavailability is crucial for fostering intimacy.

6. **Mismatched Expectations**:
   - **Overview**: Differing expectations about intimacy can lead to dissatisfaction and conflict in relationships.
   - **Key Points**: Aligning expectations through open dialogue helps in creating mutual

understanding and harmony.

**Strategies for Addressing Intimacy Issues**

1. **Improving Communication**:
   - **Practice Active Listening**:
     - **Overview**: Active listening involves fully concentrating on, understanding, and responding to what the other person is saying.
     - **Key Points**: Techniques include maintaining eye contact, nodding, summarizing, and asking clarifying questions.
   - **Expressing Needs and Feelings**:
     - **Overview**: Clearly expressing your needs and feelings helps in avoiding misunderstandings and unmet expectations.
     - **Key Points**: Use "I" statements to convey feelings and needs without blaming or criticizing the partner.
   - **Addressing Conflicts Constructively**:
     - **Overview**: Conflict resolution involves addressing disagreements in a way that strengthens rather than weakens the relationship.
     - **Key Points**: Focus on the issue, avoid personal attacks, and seek compromise and understanding.

2. **Cultivating Empathy**:
   - **Understanding Partner's Perspective**:
     - **Overview**: Empathy involves understanding and sharing the feelings of another person, which fosters emotional connection.
     - **Key Points**: Practice putting yourself

in your partner's shoes and validate their feelings.

- ◦ **Expressing Empathy**:
    - ■ **Overview**: Expressing empathy shows that you care and understand, which strengthens intimacy.
    - ■ **Key Points**: Acknowledge your partner's feelings and show support through words and actions.

3. **Building Self-Awareness**:
   - ◦ **Reflecting on Past Experiences**:
       - ■ **Overview**: Reflecting on past experiences helps in understanding how they influence current intimacy issues.
       - ■ **Key Points**: Journaling, therapy, and self-reflection can aid in this process.
   - ◦ **Identifying Patterns and Triggers**:
       - ■ **Overview**: Recognizing patterns and triggers in your behavior and emotions can help in managing intimacy challenges.
       - ■ **Key Points**: Awareness of these patterns allows for proactive changes and healthier responses.
   - ◦ **Practicing Mindfulness**:
       - ■ **Overview**: Mindfulness involves being present and aware of your thoughts, feelings, and surroundings.
       - ■ **Key Points**: Mindfulness practices, such as meditation, can enhance self-awareness and emotional regulation.

4. **Healing from Past Trauma**:
   - **Seeking Professional Support**:
     - **Overview**: Professional support, such as therapy or counseling, is often essential for healing from trauma.
     - **Key Points**: Therapists can provide strategies and tools for managing trauma-related intimacy issues.
   - **Practicing Self-Compassion**:
     - **Overview**: Self-compassion involves treating yourself with kindness and understanding in times of difficulty.
     - **Key Points**: Self-compassion promotes healing and resilience, which are crucial for overcoming intimacy barriers.

5. **Enhancing Emotional Availability**:
   - **Opening Up Gradually**:
     - **Overview**: Gradually opening up allows for the development of trust and comfort in sharing emotions.
     - **Key Points**: Start with small disclosures and build up to more significant ones as trust deepens.
   - **Prioritizing Emotional Connection**:
     - **Overview**: Making emotional connection a priority fosters intimacy.
     - **Key Points**: Engage in activities that promote emotional bonding, such as meaningful conversations and shared experiences.

6. **Aligning Expectations**:
   - **Discussing Expectations Openly**:

- **Overview**: Open discussions about expectations help in aligning them and avoiding misunderstandings.
- **Key Points**: Regularly check in with your partner about their needs and expectations regarding intimacy.

- **Setting Mutual Goals**:
  - **Overview**: Setting mutual goals for the relationship can help in creating a shared vision and understanding.
  - **Key Points**: Goals might include spending quality time together, improving communication, or addressing specific intimacy issues.

**Practical Exercises for Enhancing Intimacy**

1. **Regular Check-Ins**:
   - **Overview**: Regular check-ins involve scheduled times for partners to discuss their relationship, feelings, and any concerns.
   - **Key Points**: These check-ins promote open communication and address issues before they escalate.

2. **Mindful Touch**:
   - **Overview**: Mindful touch involves being fully present and engaged during physical touch, enhancing the connection.
   - **Key Points**: Activities like holding hands, hugging, or cuddling can be done mindfully to foster intimacy.

3. **Shared Activities**:
   - **Overview**: Engaging in shared activities strengthens bonds and creates shared memories.

- ○ **Key Points**: Choose activities that both partners enjoy and that promote interaction and connection.

4. **Empathy Exercises**:
    - ○ **Overview**: Empathy exercises help in understanding and sharing your partner's feelings.
    - ○ **Key Points**: Examples include taking turns sharing experiences and reflecting on how the other person might feel.

5. **Journaling**:
    - ○ **Overview**: Journaling about your feelings and experiences can enhance self-awareness and emotional regulation.
    - ○ **Key Points**: Reflect on your thoughts and emotions related to intimacy, and share insights with your partner if comfortable.

## Conclusion

Overcoming intimacy issues requires a combination of self-awareness, effective communication, empathy, and healing from past experiences. By identifying and addressing common barriers to intimacy, individuals and couples can build stronger, more fulfilling relationships. Practical strategies and exercises can help in enhancing intimacy and creating deeper connections.

In the next chapter, we will explore the role of gratitude in fostering intimacy. We will discuss how expressing gratitude can strengthen relationships and provide practical tips for incorporating gratitude into daily interactions. Join us as we continue our journey through the exploration of intimacy and its impact on our lives.

# CHAPTER 28: THE ROLE OF THERAPY

Therapy can be a transformative resource for individuals and couples striving to enhance their intimate relationships. It offers a structured environment where people can explore their feelings, understand their patterns, and develop healthier ways of connecting with others. This chapter delves into the role of therapy in fostering intimacy, highlighting various therapeutic approaches and their benefits.

**The Importance of Therapy in Intimate Relationships**

1. **Understanding and Resolving Conflicts**:
   - **Overview**: Therapy helps individuals and couples identify the root causes of their conflicts and provides tools for resolving them constructively.
   - **Key Points**: By addressing underlying issues, therapy can prevent recurring arguments and foster a more harmonious relationship.

2. **Improving Communication**:
   - **Overview**: Effective communication is crucial for intimacy. Therapy teaches communication skills that promote clarity, empathy, and mutual understanding.
   - **Key Points**: Therapists guide individuals and couples in expressing their needs and feelings in ways that enhance connection

rather than create distance.

3. **Building Trust and Security**:
   - **Overview**: Trust is a cornerstone of intimate relationships. Therapy can help rebuild trust after breaches and strengthen the sense of security between partners.
   - **Key Points**: Therapeutic interventions often focus on honesty, transparency, and consistent actions to restore and maintain trust.

4. **Enhancing Emotional Connection**:
   - **Overview**: Emotional intimacy involves sharing one's inner world with another person. Therapy encourages vulnerability and emotional sharing, deepening the connection between partners.
   - **Key Points**: Therapists provide a safe space for individuals to explore and express their emotions, fostering a deeper emotional bond.

## Types of Therapy for Enhancing Intimacy

1. **Individual Therapy**:
   - **Overview**: Individual therapy focuses on personal growth and self-understanding, which are crucial for healthy relationships.
   - **Key Points**: It helps individuals address personal issues, such as past trauma, self-esteem, and emotional regulation, that impact their ability to form intimate connections.

2. **Couples Therapy**:
   - **Overview**: Couples therapy addresses relational dynamics and helps partners

work together to improve their relationship.

- **Key Points**: It focuses on communication, conflict resolution, and fostering mutual respect and understanding.

3. **Family Therapy**:
    - **Overview**: Family therapy involves multiple family members and addresses the relational patterns within the family unit.
    - **Key Points**: It can help resolve family conflicts, improve communication, and foster a supportive environment for all members.

4. **Sex Therapy**:
    - **Overview**: Sex therapy addresses sexual issues and concerns that affect intimacy in relationships.
    - **Key Points**: It focuses on improving sexual communication, addressing sexual dysfunctions, and enhancing sexual satisfaction and intimacy.

5. **Group Therapy**:
    - **Overview**: Group therapy involves multiple participants who share similar issues and provides a supportive community for personal growth.
    - **Key Points**: It offers a space for individuals to share experiences, gain insights, and receive support from peers, enhancing their relational skills.

## Therapeutic Approaches

1. **Cognitive-Behavioral Therapy (CBT)**:
    - **Overview**: CBT focuses on identifying and changing negative thought patterns and

behaviors that impact relationships.

- **Key Points**: It helps individuals develop healthier thinking patterns and behaviors that promote intimacy.

2. **Emotionally Focused Therapy (EFT)**:
   - **Overview**: EFT focuses on improving emotional connection and attachment between partners.
   - **Key Points**: It helps partners identify and express their emotions, fostering a deeper emotional bond and resolving conflicts.

3. **Gottman Method**:
   - **Overview**: The Gottman Method is a structured approach to couples therapy that focuses on enhancing communication, managing conflict, and building a stronger relational foundation.
   - **Key Points**: It uses specific tools and exercises to improve relationship dynamics and foster intimacy.

4. **Psychodynamic Therapy**:
   - **Overview**: Psychodynamic therapy explores unconscious processes and how they influence behavior and relationships.
   - **Key Points**: It helps individuals understand their deeper motivations and patterns, leading to more authentic and intimate connections.

5. **Mindfulness-Based Therapy**:
   - **Overview**: Mindfulness-based therapy incorporates mindfulness practices to enhance self-awareness and emotional regulation.

- **Key Points**: It helps individuals and couples stay present in the moment, improving their ability to connect emotionally and physically.

## Benefits of Therapy for Intimacy

1. **Increased Self-Awareness**:
   - **Overview**: Therapy promotes self-reflection and self-understanding, which are essential for healthy relationships.
   - **Key Points**: Greater self-awareness helps individuals recognize their needs, emotions, and patterns, leading to more intentional and fulfilling connections.

2. **Improved Relationship Skills**:
   - **Overview**: Therapy provides tools and techniques for improving communication, conflict resolution, and emotional connection.
   - **Key Points**: These skills enhance relational satisfaction and intimacy.

3. **Healing from Past Trauma**:
   - **Overview**: Therapy helps individuals process and heal from past traumas that impact their ability to form intimate relationships.
   - **Key Points**: Healing from trauma leads to greater emotional availability and trust in relationships.

4. **Strengthened Emotional Bonds**:
   - **Overview**: Therapy encourages emotional sharing and vulnerability, which deepen emotional bonds between partners.
   - **Key Points**: Strong emotional bonds are the

foundation of intimate relationships.

5. **Enhanced Sexual Intimacy**:
   - **Overview**: Sex therapy and other therapeutic approaches address sexual issues, enhancing sexual intimacy and satisfaction.
   - **Key Points**: A healthy sexual relationship contributes to overall intimacy and relationship satisfaction.

**Practical Tips for Seeking Therapy**

1. **Finding the Right Therapist**:
   - **Overview**: It's important to find a therapist who specializes in the issues you want to address and with whom you feel comfortable.
   - **Key Points**: Research therapists, read reviews, and have initial consultations to find the right fit.

2. **Setting Clear Goals**:
   - **Overview**: Setting clear goals for therapy helps in measuring progress and staying focused.
   - **Key Points**: Discuss your goals with your therapist and regularly review them to ensure you're on track.

3. **Commitment to the Process**:
   - **Overview**: Therapy requires commitment and effort to see meaningful changes.
   - **Key Points**: Attend sessions regularly, complete any assigned homework, and stay engaged in the therapeutic process.

4. **Open Communication**:
   - **Overview**: Open communication with your

therapist is essential for effective therapy.

- ○ **Key Points**: Be honest about your feelings, progress, and any concerns you have about the therapy.

5. **Patience and Persistence**:
    - ○ **Overview**: Therapy is a process that takes time and persistence.
    - ○ **Key Points**: Be patient with yourself and the process, and stay committed to your goals.

## Conclusion

Therapy plays a crucial role in enhancing intimacy by addressing personal and relational issues, improving communication, and fostering emotional connection. Various therapeutic approaches offer different benefits, and finding the right therapist and committing to the process can lead to significant improvements in intimate relationships. In the next chapter, we will explore the role of gratitude in fostering intimacy. We will discuss how expressing gratitude can strengthen relationships and provide practical tips for incorporating gratitude into daily interactions. Join us as we continue our journey through the exploration of intimacy and its impact on our lives.

# CHAPTER 29: INTIMACY AND PERSONAL BOUNDARIES

Establishing and respecting personal boundaries is essential for cultivating healthy intimacy in relationships. Boundaries define the limits and expectations that individuals set for themselves and others, helping to maintain respect, trust, and emotional safety. This chapter explores the importance of boundaries in relationships, offering guidance on how to communicate and uphold them effectively.

**Understanding Personal Boundaries**

1. **Definition of Personal Boundaries**:
     - **Overview**: Personal boundaries are the physical, emotional, and psychological limits that individuals set to protect their well-being.

     - **Key Points**: Boundaries help individuals manage their needs, preferences, and values, fostering a sense of self-respect and mutual respect in relationships.

2. **Types of Boundaries**:
     - **Physical Boundaries**: Involve personal space, physical touch, and privacy.

- **Emotional Boundaries**: Pertains to emotional needs, feelings, and sharing personal information.
- **Intellectual Boundaries**: Relates to beliefs, ideas, and opinions.
- **Time Boundaries**: Concerns the allocation and management of personal time and commitments.
- **Material Boundaries**: Involves possessions and resources.

3. **Healthy vs. Unhealthy Boundaries**:
   - **Healthy Boundaries**: Clear, respectful, and flexible; they protect well-being while allowing for intimacy and connection.
   - **Unhealthy Boundaries**: Rigid, porous, or non-existent; they can lead to resentment, dependency, or emotional distance.

## The Importance of Boundaries in Intimate Relationships

1. **Maintaining Individuality**:
   - **Overview**: Boundaries help individuals maintain their sense of self within a relationship.
   - **Key Points**: Respecting each other's boundaries supports personal growth and prevents codependency.

2. **Fostering Mutual Respect**:
   - **Overview**: Clear boundaries promote respect for each other's needs and limits.
   - **Key Points**: They prevent misunderstandings, conflicts, and feelings of resentment.

3. **Enhancing Communication**:

- **Overview**: Discussing boundaries encourages open and honest communication.
- **Key Points**: It helps partners understand each other's expectations and preferences, leading to more effective interactions.

4. **Building Trust and Safety**:
   - **Overview**: Respecting boundaries builds trust and creates a safe emotional environment.
   - **Key Points**: It ensures that individuals feel secure in expressing their needs and vulnerabilities.

## Communicating Boundaries Effectively

1. **Self-Awareness and Reflection**:
   - **Overview**: Understanding your own boundaries requires self-awareness and reflection.
   - **Key Points**: Consider your needs, values, and limits to identify what boundaries are important to you.

2. **Clear and Assertive Communication**:
   - **Overview**: Communicate your boundaries clearly and assertively.
   - **Key Points**: Use "I" statements to express your needs and preferences without blaming or criticizing.

Examples:

- **Physical Boundaries**: "I need some personal space when I'm reading."
- **Emotional Boundaries**: "I feel uncomfortable discussing this topic right now."

- **Time Boundaries**: "I need to finish my work before we can hang out."

3. **Setting Boundaries Early**:
   - **Overview**: Establish boundaries early in the relationship to set clear expectations.
   - **Key Points**: Early boundary-setting prevents misunderstandings and sets a foundation for mutual respect.

4. **Consistency and Follow-Through**:
   - **Overview**: Be consistent in upholding your boundaries.
   - **Key Points**: Follow through with consequences if your boundaries are violated to reinforce their importance.

5. **Listening and Respecting Partner's Boundaries**:
   - **Overview**: Listen to and respect your partner's boundaries.
   - **Key Points**: Validate their needs and preferences, and be willing to adjust your behavior accordingly.

## Upholding Boundaries

1. **Recognizing Boundary Violations**:
   - **Overview**: Be aware of signs that your boundaries are being violated.
   - **Key Points**: Feelings of discomfort, resentment, or being overwhelmed can indicate boundary violations.

2. **Addressing Violations**:
   - **Overview**: Address boundary violations promptly and respectfully.
   - **Key Points**: Communicate the issue clearly and discuss how to prevent it from

happening again.

Example: "When you enter my room without knocking, I feel my privacy is not being respected. Can we agree that you'll knock first?"

3. **Re-Evaluating Boundaries**:
   - **Overview**: Boundaries may need to be re-evaluated and adjusted over time.
   - **Key Points**: Regularly check in with yourself and your partner to ensure that boundaries are still relevant and respected.

4. **Seeking Support**:
   - **Overview**: If maintaining boundaries is challenging, seek support from a therapist or counselor.
   - **Key Points**: Professional guidance can provide strategies and support for establishing and upholding boundaries.

**Practical Tips for Healthy Boundaries**

1. **Prioritize Self-Care**:
   - **Overview**: Self-care is essential for maintaining healthy boundaries.
   - **Key Points**: Take time to recharge and meet your own needs, which helps you to be more present and supportive in your relationships.

2. **Practice Saying No**:
   - **Overview**: Learn to say no to requests that violate your boundaries.
   - **Key Points**: Saying no is an important aspect of self-respect and boundary maintenance.

3. **Be Respectful and Compassionate**:
   - **Overview**: Approach boundary discussions

with respect and compassion.

- ◦ **Key Points**: Recognize that setting boundaries is a process that requires patience and understanding.

4. **Educate Yourself on Healthy Boundaries**:
    - ◦ **Overview**: Read books and resources on healthy boundaries to deepen your understanding.
    - ◦ **Key Points**: Educating yourself can provide valuable insights and strategies for boundary-setting.

## Conclusion

Establishing and respecting personal boundaries is crucial for healthy intimacy in relationships. Boundaries protect individual well-being, foster mutual respect, and enhance communication, trust, and emotional safety. By understanding the importance of boundaries, communicating them effectively, and consistently upholding them, individuals can create more fulfilling and intimate connections. In the next chapter, we will explore the role of gratitude in fostering intimacy. We will discuss how expressing gratitude can strengthen relationships and provide practical tips for incorporating gratitude into daily interactions. Join us as we continue our journey through the exploration of intimacy and its impact on our lives.

# CHAPTER 30: THE LANGUAGE OF LOVE

Understanding and expressing love in different ways is essential for fostering intimacy. The concept of love languages, introduced by Dr. Gary Chapman, highlights the different ways people give and receive love. By identifying and communicating their love languages, individuals can enhance intimacy and deepen their connections. This chapter delves into the concept of love languages, offering insights into how individuals can use them to strengthen their relationships.

**Understanding Love Languages**

1. **The Concept of Love Languages**:
    - **Overview**: Love languages are distinct ways individuals express and interpret love.
    - **Key Points**: Knowing your own love language and that of your partner can help in understanding and meeting each other's emotional needs.

2. **The Five Love Languages**:
    - **Words of Affirmation**: Expressing love through verbal compliments, appreciation, and positive encouragement.
    - **Acts of Service**: Demonstrating love through helpful actions and services that make life easier for the other person.
    - **Receiving Gifts**: Showing love through

thoughtful gifts that reflect consideration and affection.

- **Quality Time**: Spending meaningful and undivided time together, giving full attention to each other.
- **Physical Touch**: Expressing love through physical contact such as hugging, kissing, and holding hands.

## Identifying Your Love Language

1. **Self-Reflection**:
   - **Overview**: Reflect on how you feel most loved and appreciated.
   - **Key Points**: Consider past experiences and what actions or words have made you feel most valued.

2. **Taking the Love Language Quiz**:
   - **Overview**: Dr. Gary Chapman's love language quiz can help identify your primary love language.
   - **Key Points**: The quiz provides insights into your preferred way of receiving love, which can guide your interactions.

3. **Observing Your Reactions**:
   - **Overview**: Pay attention to your reactions to different expressions of love.
   - **Key Points**: Notice what makes you feel happiest and most connected in your relationships.

## Communicating Your Love Language

1. **Open Discussion with Partner**:
   - **Overview**: Discuss your love languages with your partner.

- **Key Points**: Sharing your love language helps your partner understand how to make you feel loved and appreciated.

2. **Expressing Your Needs**:
    - **Overview**: Clearly express your needs and preferences to your partner.
    - **Key Points**: Use "I" statements to communicate your love language without making your partner feel inadequate.

Example: "I feel really loved when you spend quality time with me."

3. **Mutual Understanding**:
    - **Overview**: Aim for a mutual understanding of each other's love languages.
    - **Key Points**: Respect each other's preferences and make a conscious effort to meet them.

## Enhancing Intimacy Through Love Languages

1. **Adapting Your Actions**:
    - **Overview**: Adapt your actions to align with your partner's love language.
    - **Key Points**: Small adjustments in your behavior can significantly enhance intimacy and satisfaction in the relationship.

2. **Consistency and Effort**:
    - **Overview**: Consistently express love in ways that resonate with your partner's love language.
    - **Key Points**: Regular and thoughtful gestures reinforce feelings of love and connection.

3. **Being Open to Change**:
    - **Overview**: Love languages can evolve over time.

- **Key Points**: Be open to revisiting and adjusting your expressions of love as your relationship grows and changes.

## Common Challenges and Solutions

1. **Different Love Languages**:
   - **Challenge**: Partners with different love languages may struggle to feel understood and appreciated.
   - **Solution**: Educate yourselves on each other's love languages and make intentional efforts to express love in ways that resonate with your partner.

2. **Miscommunication**:
   - **Challenge**: Misunderstandings can arise if love languages are not clearly communicated.
   - **Solution**: Engage in regular and open conversations about how each of you feels most loved and appreciated.

3. **Inconsistency**:
   - **Challenge**: Inconsistency in expressing love can lead to feelings of neglect.
   - **Solution**: Make a conscious effort to incorporate your partner's love language into daily interactions consistently.

## Practical Tips for Using Love Languages

1. **Words of Affirmation**:
   - **Tips**: Regularly compliment and express appreciation. Leave thoughtful notes or messages to brighten your partner's day.

2. **Acts of Service**:
   - **Tips**: Offer to help with tasks or chores. Look

for ways to make your partner's life easier and show consideration.

3. **Receiving Gifts**:
    - **Tips**: Give thoughtful and meaningful gifts, regardless of their monetary value. Pay attention to special occasions and surprises.

4. **Quality Time**:
    - **Tips**: Plan activities that allow for undivided attention. Schedule regular date nights or quality time sessions.

5. **Physical Touch**:
    - **Tips**: Incorporate physical affection into your daily routine. Hold hands, hug, and offer comforting touches.

## Conclusion

Understanding and expressing love in different ways is essential for fostering intimacy. By identifying and communicating love languages, individuals can enhance their connections and deepen their relationships. In the next chapter, we will explore the concept of gratitude and its role in fostering intimacy. We will discuss how expressing gratitude can strengthen relationships and provide practical tips for incorporating gratitude into daily interactions. Join us as we continue our journey through the exploration of intimacy and its impact on our lives.

# CHAPTER 31: INTIMACY IN CRISIS SITUATIONS

Crises can test the strength of intimate relationships, introducing stress and uncertainty that can either strain or strengthen the bond between partners. Whether dealing with personal issues, health problems, financial difficulties, or external events, the way couples navigate these challenges plays a crucial role in maintaining and deepening their intimacy. This chapter explores how to maintain and strengthen intimacy during difficult times, offering strategies for coping and supporting each other.

**Understanding the Impact of Crisis on Intimacy**

1. **Types of Crises**:
   - **Personal Crises**: Job loss, health issues, grief, or emotional trauma.
   - **Relational Crises**: Infidelity, major disagreements, or unmet expectations.
   - **External Crises**: Natural disasters, economic downturns, or societal upheavals.

2. **Emotional Reactions to Crisis**:
   - **Stress and Anxiety**: Elevated stress levels can lead to anxiety, irritability, and conflict.
   - **Fear and Uncertainty**: Fear of the unknown can cause withdrawal and isolation.

- **Resilience and Growth**: Crises can also foster resilience, leading to personal and relational growth.

**Strategies for Maintaining Intimacy During Crisis**

1. **Open and Honest Communication**:
   - **Express Feelings**: Share your thoughts and emotions openly with your partner.
   - **Active Listening**: Listen to your partner's concerns without judgment or interruption.
   - **Regular Check-Ins**: Schedule regular discussions to address ongoing concerns and provide emotional support.

2. **Emotional Support and Empathy**:
   - **Be Present**: Offer your presence and attention to your partner during difficult times.
   - **Show Empathy**: Validate your partner's feelings and experiences, showing understanding and compassion.
   - **Provide Reassurance**: Offer words of reassurance and comfort to alleviate fears and uncertainties.

3. **Collaborative Problem-Solving**:
   - **Work as a Team**: Approach challenges as a united front, collaborating on solutions.
   - **Set Priorities**: Identify and prioritize the most pressing issues to address together.
   - **Seek Compromise**: Be willing to compromise and find mutually acceptable solutions.

4. **Maintain Physical Connection**:
   - **Non-Sexual Touch**: Hugging, holding

hands, and other forms of non-sexual touch can provide comfort and reassurance.

- **Intimate Time**: Make time for physical intimacy, even if it's just holding each other.
- **Affectionate Gestures**: Small acts of affection can help maintain a sense of closeness.

5. **Self-Care and Individual Resilience**:
   - **Personal Well-Being**: Take care of your own physical and emotional health to be better equipped to support your partner.
   - **Stress Management**: Engage in activities that help reduce stress, such as exercise, meditation, or hobbies.
   - **Seek Support**: Don't hesitate to seek external support from friends, family, or professionals if needed.

## Navigating Specific Crisis Situations

1. **Health Crises**:
   - **Medical Support**: Ensure access to necessary medical care and support.
   - **Emotional Support**: Provide emotional support and be a source of strength for your partner.
   - **Practical Help**: Assist with daily tasks and responsibilities to ease the burden.

2. **Financial Crises**:
   - **Budgeting**: Work together to create a budget and manage finances effectively.
   - **Resourcefulness**: Explore alternative income sources or ways to reduce expenses.
   - **Mutual Support**: Offer emotional support

and understanding, avoiding blame or criticism.

3. **Relational Crises**:
   - **Counseling**: Consider seeking couples therapy to address underlying issues and improve communication.
   - **Rebuilding Trust**: Focus on rebuilding trust through consistent actions and transparency.
   - **Forgiveness**: Work towards forgiveness and healing to move past relational wounds.

4. **External Crises**:
   - **Stay Informed**: Keep informed about the situation and take necessary precautions.
   - **Community Support**: Engage with community resources and support networks.
   - **Focus on Togetherness**: Prioritize time together to strengthen your bond amidst external challenges.

## Building Resilience for Future Crises

1. **Developing Coping Strategies**:
   - **Identify Strengths**: Recognize and build on your individual and relational strengths.
   - **Learn from Experience**: Reflect on past crises and the strategies that helped you cope.
   - **Prepare for the Future**: Develop a plan for potential future crises, ensuring you are better prepared.

2. **Strengthening the Relationship**:
   - **Regular Communication**: Maintain open

and honest communication as a foundation of your relationship.

- **Shared Goals**: Establish shared goals and values that guide you through challenges.
- **Continual Growth**: Commit to continual personal and relational growth, fostering resilience and adaptability.

3. **Seeking Professional Help**:

- **Therapy and Counseling**: Engage in therapy or counseling to address ongoing issues and develop coping mechanisms.
- **Support Groups**: Join support groups for individuals or couples facing similar challenges.
- **Educational Resources**: Utilize books, workshops, and other resources to enhance your understanding and skills.

## Conclusion

Crises can test the strength of intimate relationships but also offer opportunities for growth and deeper connection. By maintaining open communication, providing emotional support, collaborating on solutions, and prioritizing physical connection, couples can navigate difficult times together and emerge stronger. In the next chapter, we will explore the role of gratitude in fostering intimacy. We will discuss how expressing gratitude can strengthen relationships and provide practical tips for incorporating gratitude into daily interactions. Join us as we continue our journey through the exploration of intimacy and its impact on our lives.

# CHAPTER 32: INTIMACY IN TIMES OF CHANGE

Life is full of changes, whether they are planned or unexpected. Moving to a new place, transitioning in careers, dealing with health issues, or even experiencing significant life milestones can all impact intimacy in relationships. During these times of change, maintaining intimate connections can be challenging but also incredibly rewarding. This chapter discusses how to navigate changes while maintaining intimate connections, emphasizing the importance of flexibility and communication.

**Understanding the Impact of Change on Intimacy**

1. **Types of Changes**:
    - **Geographical Relocations**: Moving to a new city, state, or country.
    - **Career Transitions**: Starting a new job, changing careers, or retiring.
    - **Health Issues**: Coping with illness, injury, or changes in physical or mental health.
    - **Life Milestones**: Marriage, having children, empty nesting, or personal achievements.

2. **Emotional Responses to Change**:
    - **Stress and Anxiety**: Uncertainty and disruption can lead to increased stress and

anxiety.

- **Excitement and Hope**: Positive changes can bring excitement and a sense of renewal.
- **Fear of the Unknown**: Changes often bring fear of the unknown and discomfort with new situations.

**Strategies for Maintaining Intimacy During Change**

1. **Open and Honest Communication**:
   - **Express Feelings**: Share your thoughts and emotions about the change with your partner.
   - **Active Listening**: Listen to your partner's concerns and feelings without judgment.
   - **Regular Check-Ins**: Schedule regular discussions to address ongoing concerns and provide emotional support.

2. **Flexibility and Adaptability**:
   - **Be Open to Change**: Embrace the change and be willing to adapt as needed.
   - **Adjust Expectations**: Understand that routines and dynamics may shift, and adjust your expectations accordingly.
   - **Find New Norms**: Create new routines and norms that work in the new circumstances.

3. **Emotional Support and Empathy**:
   - **Be Present**: Offer your presence and attention to your partner during times of change.
   - **Show Empathy**: Validate your partner's feelings and experiences, showing understanding and compassion.
   - **Provide Reassurance**: Offer words of

reassurance and comfort to alleviate fears and uncertainties.

4. **Maintaining Physical Connection**:
    - **Non-Sexual Touch**: Hugging, holding hands, and other forms of non-sexual touch can provide comfort and reassurance.
    - **Intimate Time**: Make time for physical intimacy, even if it's just holding each other.
    - **Affectionate Gestures**: Small acts of affection can help maintain a sense of closeness.

5. **Self-Care and Individual Resilience**:
    - **Personal Well-Being**: Take care of your own physical and emotional health to be better equipped to support your partner.
    - **Stress Management**: Engage in activities that help reduce stress, such as exercise, meditation, or hobbies.
    - **Seek Support**: Don't hesitate to seek external support from friends, family, or professionals if needed.

**Navigating Specific Changes**

1. **Geographical Relocations**:
    - **Explore Together**: Discover new places and activities together to create shared experiences.
    - **Stay Connected**: Use technology to stay connected with old friends while building new connections in your new location.
    - **Create a Home**: Work together to make your new place feel like home, creating a safe and comfortable environment.

2. **Career Transitions**:
    - **Support Each Other**: Be supportive of each other's career changes and the associated stresses.
    - **Balance Work and Life**: Find a balance between work and personal life to ensure time for intimacy.
    - **Celebrate Achievements**: Celebrate each other's career milestones and achievements, no matter how small.

3. **Health Issues**:
    - **Provide Care**: Be there for each other, offering care and support during health challenges.
    - **Adjust Activities**: Adjust your activities and routines to accommodate health needs while still finding ways to connect.
    - **Seek Help**: Don't hesitate to seek professional help or join support groups for additional support.

4. **Life Milestones**:
    - **Celebrate Together**: Celebrate significant life milestones together, creating memories and shared experiences.
    - **Support Growth**: Support each other's personal growth and changes that come with life milestones.
    - **Plan for the Future**: Discuss and plan for the future together, aligning your goals and aspirations.

**Building Resilience for Future Changes**

1. **Developing Coping Strategies**:
    - **Identify Strengths**: Recognize and build on

your individual and relational strengths.

- **Learn from Experience**: Reflect on past changes and the strategies that helped you cope.
- **Prepare for the Future**: Develop a plan for potential future changes, ensuring you are better prepared.

2.  **Strengthening the Relationship**:
    - **Regular Communication**: Maintain open and honest communication as a foundation of your relationship.
    - **Shared Goals**: Establish shared goals and values that guide you through changes.
    - **Continual Growth**: Commit to continual personal and relational growth, fostering resilience and adaptability.

3.  **Seeking Professional Help**:
    - **Therapy and Counseling**: Engage in therapy or counseling to address ongoing issues and develop coping mechanisms.
    - **Support Groups**: Join support groups for individuals or couples facing similar changes.
    - **Educational Resources**: Utilize books, workshops, and other resources to enhance your understanding and skills.

## Conclusion

Times of change can test the strength of intimate relationships, but they also offer opportunities for growth and deeper connection. By maintaining open communication, being flexible and adaptable, providing emotional support, and prioritizing physical connection, couples can navigate changes together and emerge stronger. In the next chapter, we will explore the role of gratitude in fostering intimacy. We will discuss how expressing gratitude can strengthen relationships and provide practical tips for incorporating gratitude into daily interactions. Join us as we continue our journey through the exploration of intimacy and its impact on our lives.

# CHAPTER 33:
# SPIRITUAL INTIMACY

Spiritual intimacy is a profound and often overlooked aspect of relationships. It involves sharing beliefs, values, and practices with another person, fostering a deep connection that transcends the physical and emotional. Spiritual intimacy can enhance the overall bond between partners, providing a sense of purpose, unity, and shared meaning. This chapter explores the role of spirituality in fostering deep connections and offers tips for cultivating spiritual intimacy.

**Understanding Spiritual Intimacy**

1. **Definition and Scope**:
    - **Shared Beliefs**: Common religious or spiritual beliefs that create a sense of unity and purpose.
    - **Values and Principles**: Shared values and principles that guide actions and decisions.
    - **Spiritual Practices**: Engaging in spiritual practices together, such as prayer, meditation, or worship.

2. **Components of Spiritual Intimacy**:
    - **Connection with the Divine**: A mutual connection with a higher power or the universe.
    - **Shared Moral Framework**: Common ethical and moral guidelines that shape behavior.

- **Mutual Respect and Understanding**: Respecting and understanding each other's spiritual perspectives and practices.

## The Role of Spirituality in Fostering Deep Connections

1. **Creating a Sense of Purpose**:
   - **Unified Goals**: Sharing a spiritual journey can create unified goals and a sense of shared destiny.
   - **Meaningful Conversations**: Engaging in deep, meaningful conversations about spirituality can enhance emotional and intellectual intimacy.

2. **Strengthening Emotional Bonds**:
   - **Support and Encouragement**: Providing spiritual support and encouragement during difficult times can strengthen emotional bonds.
   - **Shared Experiences**: Participating in spiritual activities together creates shared experiences that deepen the connection.

3. **Enhancing Trust and Respect**:
   - **Respecting Differences**: Respecting each other's spiritual beliefs fosters mutual respect and trust.
   - **Honoring Commitments**: Living according to shared spiritual values reinforces trust and commitment.

## Cultivating Spiritual Intimacy

1. **Open and Honest Communication**:
   - **Discuss Beliefs and Values**: Have open discussions about your spiritual beliefs, values, and practices.
   - **Listen Actively**: Listen to your partner's

spiritual experiences and perspectives without judgment.

- **Be Vulnerable**: Share your spiritual struggles and doubts, fostering deeper understanding and connection.

2. **Engaging in Spiritual Practices Together**:
   - **Pray or Meditate Together**: Engage in prayer or meditation as a couple, creating a sense of unity and peace.
   - **Attend Services**: Participate in religious or spiritual services together.
   - **Celebrate Rituals**: Celebrate spiritual rituals and traditions together, creating shared memories and experiences.

3. **Supporting Each Other's Spiritual Growth**:
   - **Encourage Exploration**: Encourage each other to explore and deepen your spiritual journeys.
   - **Read and Study Together**: Read spiritual texts or attend study groups together.
   - **Respect Individual Paths**: Respect and support each other's individual spiritual paths, even if they differ.

4. **Creating a Spiritual Environment**:
   - **Sacred Space**: Create a sacred space in your home for spiritual practices and reflection.
   - **Symbols and Art**: Incorporate spiritual symbols and art that reflect your shared beliefs and values.
   - **Daily Practices**: Establish daily spiritual practices that you can do together, such as gratitude rituals or morning prayers.

5. **Seeking Guidance and Wisdom**:
    - **Mentors and Leaders**: Seek guidance from spiritual mentors or leaders who can provide wisdom and support.
    - **Community Involvement**: Get involved in a spiritual community that supports and nurtures your spiritual intimacy.
    - **Continual Learning**: Continually seek knowledge and understanding through books, workshops, and retreats.

## Overcoming Challenges in Spiritual Intimacy

1. **Differing Beliefs and Practices**:
    - **Respect and Tolerance**: Practice respect and tolerance for each other's differing beliefs and practices.
    - **Find Common Ground**: Identify and focus on common spiritual values and practices that you both share.
    - **Create New Traditions**: Create new spiritual traditions that incorporate elements from both partners' beliefs.

2. **Balancing Individual and Shared Spirituality**:
    - **Personal Time**: Allow time for individual spiritual practices and reflection.
    - **Shared Activities**: Balance individual spirituality with shared spiritual activities and experiences.
    - **Support Independence**: Support each other's independent spiritual growth and exploration.

3. **Navigating Spiritual Crises**:
    - **Provide Support**: Offer support and understanding during spiritual crises or

periods of doubt.

- **Seek Guidance**: Seek guidance from spiritual leaders or mentors during challenging times.
- **Stay Connected**: Maintain open communication and stay connected, even during spiritual struggles.

## Conclusion

Spiritual intimacy is a powerful and enriching aspect of relationships, providing a deep sense of connection, purpose, and unity. By sharing beliefs, values, and practices, couples can foster a spiritual bond that enhances their overall relationship. In the next chapter, we will explore the role of gratitude in fostering intimacy. We will discuss how expressing gratitude can strengthen relationships and provide practical tips for incorporating gratitude into daily interactions. Join us as we continue our journey through the exploration of intimacy and its impact on our lives.

# CHAPTER 34: INTIMACY AND CREATIVITY

Creativity is a powerful tool for enhancing intimacy in relationships. It provides unique ways to connect, express emotions, and deepen bonds between partners. Engaging in creative activities together can foster a sense of playfulness, collaboration, and mutual understanding. This chapter explores the relationship between intimacy and creativity, offering suggestions for incorporating creative activities into relationships to strengthen connections.

**Understanding the Connection Between Intimacy and Creativity**

1. **Creativity as Expression**:
    - **Emotional Outlet**: Creativity allows individuals to express their emotions in unique and personal ways.
    - **Communication Tool**: Creative activities can serve as a medium for communicating feelings that might be difficult to express verbally.

2. **Creativity as Collaboration**:
    - **Shared Projects**: Working on creative projects together fosters teamwork and cooperation.

- **Problem-Solving**: Creative activities often involve problem-solving, which can enhance cognitive and emotional intimacy.

3. **Creativity as Play**:
    - **Playfulness**: Engaging in creative play can bring joy and laughter into the relationship, reducing stress and increasing bonding.
    - **Exploration**: Creativity encourages exploration and experimentation, allowing couples to discover new facets of each other and their relationship.

## Benefits of Incorporating Creativity into Relationships

1. **Enhanced Communication**:
    - **Non-Verbal Expression**: Creative activities like painting, music, or dance allow for non-verbal expression of emotions.
    - **Shared Language**: Developing a shared language through creative expression can deepen understanding and empathy.

2. **Increased Emotional Intimacy**:
    - **Vulnerability**: Sharing creative work can be a vulnerable act, fostering deeper emotional connections.
    - **Shared Experiences**: Creating something together builds shared memories and experiences that strengthen emotional bonds.

3. **Strengthened Physical Intimacy**:
    - **Touch and Proximity**: Many creative activities involve physical closeness, such as dancing or crafting.
    - **Sensory Engagement**: Engaging the senses through creative activities can enhance

physical intimacy and connection.

4. **Enhanced Problem-Solving Skills**:
    - **Collaborative Efforts**: Working together on creative projects can improve problem-solving skills and cooperation.
    - **Innovative Thinking**: Creativity encourages innovative thinking, which can be applied to resolving conflicts and challenges in the relationship.

## Creative Activities to Enhance Intimacy

1. **Art and Craft Projects**:
    - **Painting or Drawing**: Create artwork together, expressing emotions and ideas through visual art.
    - **Crafting**: Engage in DIY projects, making something meaningful together.

2. **Music and Dance**:
    - **Playing Instruments**: Learn to play musical instruments together or create music as a duo.
    - **Dancing**: Take dance classes or simply dance together at home, enjoying the physical closeness and rhythm.

3. **Writing and Storytelling**:
    - **Writing Letters**: Write love letters or notes to each other, expressing feelings and thoughts.
    - **Storytelling**: Create stories together, taking turns to add to the narrative.

4. **Cooking and Baking**:
    - **Recipe Creation**: Invent new recipes together, experimenting with different ingredients and flavors.

- **Cooking Together**: Prepare meals as a team, enjoying the process and the shared result.

5. **Photography and Filmmaking**:
   - **Photo Projects**: Take photos together, capturing moments and creating visual memories.
   - **Video Projects**: Make short films or videos together, documenting experiences or creating fictional stories.

6. **Gardening and Nature Activities**:
   - **Gardening**: Plant and nurture a garden together, enjoying the process of growth and the beauty of nature.
   - **Outdoor Adventures**: Engage in outdoor activities like hiking, camping, or picnicking, exploring and connecting with nature.

**Tips for Incorporating Creativity into Relationships**

1. **Create a Safe Space**:
   - **Encourage Expression**: Foster an environment where both partners feel comfortable expressing themselves creatively.
   - **Be Supportive**: Offer encouragement and support for each other's creative efforts.

2. **Schedule Regular Creative Time**:
   - **Set Aside Time**: Dedicate regular time for creative activities, making it a priority in the relationship.
   - **Be Consistent**: Consistency helps build a routine and ensures that creative activities become a regular part of your relationship.

3. **Be Open to Experimentation**:

- **Try New Things**: Be willing to try new creative activities and step out of your comfort zone.
- **Embrace Imperfection**: Understand that creativity is not about perfection but about expression and connection.

4. **Celebrate Achievements**:
   - **Acknowledge Efforts**: Celebrate the effort and process, not just the final product.
   - **Share Creations**: Share your creative work with each other and with others, if comfortable, to reinforce the bond.

**Overcoming Challenges in Creative Intimacy**

1. **Dealing with Different Interests**:
   - **Find Common Ground**: Identify creative activities that both partners enjoy or are willing to try.
   - **Respect Individual Preferences**: Allow space for individual creative pursuits while also finding ways to collaborate.

2. **Managing Time and Resources**:
   - **Prioritize Activities**: Make creative activities a priority by scheduling them into your routine.
   - **Use Available Resources**: Be resourceful with what you have, making use of available materials and tools.

3. **Addressing Self-Doubt and Insecurity**:
   - **Encourage Each Other**: Offer positive reinforcement and encouragement to build confidence.
   - **Focus on Process**: Emphasize the joy of the creative process rather than the outcome.

## Conclusion

Creativity is a powerful tool for enhancing intimacy, providing unique ways to connect and express emotions. By incorporating creative activities into your relationship, you can foster deeper emotional, physical, and intellectual connections. In the next chapter, we will explore the role of gratitude in fostering intimacy. We will discuss how expressing gratitude can strengthen relationships and provide practical tips for incorporating gratitude into daily interactions. Join us as we continue our journey through the exploration of intimacy and its impact on our lives.

# CHAPTER 35: DEVELOPING INTIMACY SKILLS

Intimacy is not just a natural byproduct of relationships but also a skill that can be developed and refined. By focusing on communication, empathy, and emotional expression, individuals can enhance their ability to connect deeply with others. This chapter provides practical exercises and techniques for developing these intimacy skills, offering a roadmap for cultivating stronger and more meaningful relationships.

**Understanding Intimacy Skills**

1. **Definition and Importance**:
   - **Intimacy Skills**: Techniques and practices that enhance emotional closeness, trust, and mutual understanding in relationships.
   - **Impact**: Improved intimacy skills contribute to stronger, more fulfilling relationships by fostering open communication, empathy, and emotional connection.

2. **Core Areas**:
   - **Communication**: Effective verbal and non-verbal communication that facilitates understanding and connection.

- **Empathy**: The ability to understand and share the feelings of another person.
- **Emotional Expression**: The capacity to express and manage emotions in a healthy and constructive manner.

## Enhancing Communication Skills

1. **Active Listening**:
   - **Practice**: Fully engage with your partner when they are speaking. Avoid interrupting and focus on understanding their perspective.
   - **Techniques**: Use reflective listening by paraphrasing what the other person has said and asking clarifying questions to ensure comprehension.

2. **Effective Verbal Communication**:
   - **Clarity**: Be clear and concise when expressing your thoughts and feelings. Avoid vague language or assumptions.
   - **Assertiveness**: Communicate your needs and boundaries assertively while respecting the other person's needs and boundaries.

3. **Non-Verbal Communication**:
   - **Body Language**: Pay attention to your body language and facial expressions. Ensure they align with your verbal messages.
   - **Physical Touch**: Use appropriate physical touch to convey warmth and support, enhancing the connection between partners.

4. **Regular Check-Ins**:
   - **Scheduled Conversations**: Set aside regular times to discuss feelings, concerns, and

updates in the relationship.

- **Feedback**: Offer and request feedback on communication patterns and areas for improvement.

**Cultivating Empathy**

1. **Empathic Listening**:
   - **Listening Without Judgment**: Listen to your partner's experiences and emotions without making judgments or offering immediate solutions.
   - **Emotional Resonance**: Tune into the emotions behind their words and acknowledge their feelings.

2. **Perspective-Taking**:
   - **Role Reversal**: Imagine yourself in your partner's position to better understand their point of view.
   - **Ask Open-Ended Questions**: Encourage your partner to share more about their experiences and feelings through open-ended questions.

3. **Validation**:
   - **Acknowledge Feelings**: Validate your partner's emotions by acknowledging their experiences and expressing understanding.
   - **Supportive Responses**: Offer supportive responses that show you are emotionally present and engaged.

4. **Empathy Exercises**:
   - **Journaling**: Write about your own and your partner's feelings and perspectives to deepen your understanding.
   - **Role-Playing**: Engage in role-playing

exercises to practice responding empathetically in various scenarios.

**Mastering Emotional Expression**

1. **Identifying Emotions**:
   - **Self-Awareness**: Develop awareness of your own emotions by checking in with yourself regularly.
   - **Emotion Vocabulary**: Expand your vocabulary to accurately describe your feelings and experiences.

2. **Expressing Emotions Constructively**:
   - **Use "I" Statements**: Express your emotions using "I" statements to take ownership of your feelings and avoid blaming or criticizing.
   - **Describe and Share**: Clearly describe your emotions and share how they affect you, providing context and insights.

3. **Managing Emotions**:
   - **Emotional Regulation**: Use techniques such as deep breathing, mindfulness, or journaling to manage and regulate your emotions.
   - **Seek Support**: If needed, seek support from a therapist or counselor to address emotional challenges.

4. **Practice Exercises**:
   - **Daily Check-Ins**: Regularly check in with yourself and your partner about how you are feeling and how it is affecting your relationship.
   - **Emotional Sharing**: Share personal experiences and emotions with your

partner, encouraging them to do the same.

**Practical Exercises for Developing Intimacy Skills**

1. **Communication Exercise: The "Check-In" Ritual**:
   - **Frequency**: Set a regular time each week for a "check-in" conversation.
   - **Structure**: Discuss your feelings, any concerns, and positive experiences. Use active listening and ensure both partners have equal opportunities to speak.

2. **Empathy Exercise: The "Perspective-Taking" Challenge**:
   - **Task**: For a week, focus on understanding your partner's perspective in various situations.
   - **Reflect**: At the end of the week, share your insights and discuss how this exercise impacted your understanding and connection.

3. **Emotional Expression Exercise: The "Emotion Journal"**:
   - **Daily Practice**: Keep a daily journal where you write about your emotions and their triggers.
   - **Sharing**: Share selected entries with your partner to foster openness and understanding.

4. **Couples' Creativity Exercise: The "Joint Project"**:
   - **Choose a Project**: Select a creative project, such as a DIY craft, cooking a new recipe, or making art together.
   - **Collaborate**: Work on the project together, focusing on communication, collaboration, and expressing emotions through the

creative process.

## Overcoming Challenges in Developing Intimacy Skills

1. **Resistance to Change**:
     - **Patience and Persistence**: Understand that developing intimacy skills takes time and practice. Be patient with yourself and your partner.
     - **Positive Reinforcement**: Celebrate small successes and improvements to encourage continued growth.

2. **Conflicting Communication Styles**:
     - **Adaptation**: Be open to adapting your communication style to better align with your partner's style.
     - **Compromise**: Find a middle ground that allows both partners to feel heard and understood.

3. **Emotional Vulnerability**:
     - **Create Safe Spaces**: Build a safe and supportive environment where both partners feel comfortable expressing their emotions.
     - **Seek Support**: If necessary, seek guidance from a therapist to address issues related to emotional vulnerability.

## Conclusion

Developing intimacy skills is a continuous process that requires commitment, practice, and openness. By focusing on communication, empathy, and emotional expression, individuals can enhance their ability to connect deeply with others and build stronger, more fulfilling relationships. In the next chapter, we will explore the role of forgiveness in relationships. We will discuss how forgiveness can heal and strengthen connections and offer practical strategies for incorporating forgiveness into daily interactions. Join us as we continue our journey through the exploration of intimacy and its impact on our lives.

# CHAPTER 36: THE INFLUENCE OF FAMILY DYNAMICS

Family dynamics significantly shape individuals' perceptions and experiences of intimacy. The relationships we have with our family members can influence our ability to form and maintain intimate connections in other areas of our lives. This chapter explores the impact of family relationships on intimacy, highlighting how family dynamics can affect our approach to relationships and offering strategies for overcoming familial challenges.

**Understanding Family Dynamics**

1. **Definition and Scope**:
    - **Family Dynamics**: The patterns of interaction, communication, and relationships among family members.

    - **Influence on Intimacy**: Family dynamics can shape our beliefs about intimacy, affect our emotional and relational skills, and impact our expectations in intimate relationships.

2. **Types of Family Dynamics**:
    - **Healthy Dynamics**: Families characterized by open communication, support, and mutual respect.

- ◦ **Dysfunctional Dynamics**: Families with patterns of conflict, control, neglect, or enmeshment.

## Impact of Family Dynamics on Intimacy

1. **Early Attachments and Relationships**:
   - ◦ **Attachment Theory**: Early relationships with caregivers form the basis for attachment styles, which influence how we relate to others in intimate relationships.
   - ◦ **Secure Attachments**: Positive early experiences foster trust and healthy intimacy in later relationships.
   - ◦ **Insecure Attachments**: Negative early experiences can lead to difficulties in forming secure and trusting relationships.

2. **Family Communication Patterns**:
   - ◦ **Open Communication**: Families that model open and honest communication tend to produce individuals who are comfortable expressing their feelings and needs in relationships.
   - ◦ **Closed or Dysfunctional Communication**: Families with poor communication patterns may result in individuals who struggle with expressing emotions and addressing conflicts.

3. **Role Models and Expectations**:
   - ◦ **Healthy Role Models**: Positive family role models demonstrate effective intimacy skills, such as empathy, respect, and support.
   - ◦ **Negative Role Models**: Dysfunctional family role models may perpetuate unhealthy

relationship patterns and unrealistic expectations of intimacy.

4. **Conflict Resolution and Coping Skills**:
    - **Effective Conflict Resolution**: Families that model constructive conflict resolution teach individuals how to handle disagreements and maintain intimacy.
    - **Ineffective Conflict Resolution**: Families that model conflict avoidance or aggression may lead to challenges in managing conflicts in intimate relationships.

5. **Cultural and Familial Values**:
    - **Cultural Influences**: Family values and cultural norms shape our beliefs about intimacy and influence how we approach relationships.
    - **Familial Expectations**: Expectations set by family members can impact how individuals view intimacy and their willingness to engage in certain types of relationships.

## Addressing Familial Challenges

1. **Identifying and Understanding Patterns**:
    - **Self-Reflection**: Reflect on your family dynamics and how they may have influenced your views and behaviors regarding intimacy.
    - **Pattern Recognition**: Identify recurring patterns or themes in your family relationships that may impact your current relationships.

2. **Seeking Professional Help**:
    - **Therapy**: Engage in individual or family

therapy to address unresolved issues and work through familial challenges affecting intimacy.

- **Counseling**: Seek counseling to develop healthier relationship patterns and enhance your ability to form and maintain intimate connections.

3. **Setting Healthy Boundaries**:
   - **Define Boundaries**: Establish clear and respectful boundaries with family members to protect your own emotional well-being.

   - **Communicate Boundaries**: Clearly communicate your boundaries and expectations to family members to foster healthier interactions.

4. **Developing Positive Relationships**:
   - **Build Supportive Connections**: Cultivate relationships with individuals who support your personal growth and intimacy goals.

   - **Seek Positive Role Models**: Surround yourself with people who model healthy intimacy and relationship skills.

5. **Enhancing Communication Skills**:
   - **Practice Effective Communication**: Use active listening, assertiveness, and empathy to improve communication with family members and in your intimate relationships.

   - **Address Conflicts Constructively**: Approach conflicts with a problem-solving mindset and work towards resolution rather than avoidance.

6. **Building Emotional Resilience**:

- **Self-Care**: Engage in self-care practices to maintain emotional health and resilience in the face of familial challenges.

- **Support Systems**: Build a support network of friends, mentors, or support groups to help you navigate familial issues and strengthen your intimacy skills.

**Practical Exercises for Improving Family Dynamics**

1. **Family Communication Exercise: The "Family Meeting"**:
   - **Frequency**: Schedule regular family meetings to discuss feelings, concerns, and updates.
   - **Structure**: Use a structured format to ensure everyone has an opportunity to speak and be heard.

2. **Boundary Setting Exercise: The "Boundary Mapping"**:
   - **Task**: Create a visual map of your personal boundaries and discuss them with family members.
   - **Review**: Regularly review and adjust boundaries as needed to maintain healthy relationships.

3. **Conflict Resolution Exercise: The "Role-Playing" Scenario**:
   - **Task**: Role-play common conflict scenarios with a trusted friend or therapist to practice constructive resolution strategies.
   - **Feedback**: Discuss the outcomes and receive feedback on your conflict resolution skills.

4. **Self-Reflection Exercise: The "Family Influence Journal"**:

- **Daily Practice**: Keep a journal to reflect on how family dynamics influence your current relationships and intimacy.

- **Insights**: Use the journal to gain insights into patterns and develop strategies for improvement.

5. **Positive Relationship Exercise: The "Support Network Building"**:

   - **Task**: Identify and build relationships with individuals who provide positive support and encouragement.

   - **Engage**: Actively engage with your support network to foster healthy and supportive connections.

## Conclusion

Family dynamics play a crucial role in shaping our experiences and understanding of intimacy. By examining the impact of family relationships on our intimate connections and addressing familial challenges, we can develop healthier patterns and enhance our ability to form and maintain meaningful relationships. In the next chapter, we will explore the concept of forgiveness in relationships. We will discuss how forgiveness can heal and strengthen connections and offer practical strategies for incorporating forgiveness into daily interactions. Join us as we continue our journey through the exploration of intimacy and its impact on our lives.

# CHAPTER 37: INTIMACY IN THE WORKPLACE

Workplace relationships often encompass various levels of intimacy, ranging from professional camaraderie to more personal connections. Navigating intimacy in the workplace requires a balance between fostering meaningful connections and maintaining professionalism. This chapter explores the nuances of workplace intimacy, emphasizing the importance of boundaries and professionalism while acknowledging the benefits of positive workplace relationships.

**Understanding Workplace Intimacy**

1. **Definition and Scope**:
    - **Workplace Intimacy**: The degree of personal connection and emotional closeness that develops between colleagues. It includes aspects of camaraderie, mutual support, and personal sharing.
    - **Types**: Relationships in the workplace can vary from purely professional to more personal, including friendships, mentorships, and, in some cases, romantic relationships.

2. **The Role of Intimacy**:
    - **Positive Impact**: Positive workplace relationships can enhance job satisfaction,

collaboration, and overall morale.

- **Potential Challenges**: Intimacy can also lead to conflicts, favoritism, and ethical dilemmas if not managed appropriately.

## Benefits of Workplace Intimacy

1. **Enhanced Collaboration**:
   - **Team Building**: Strong interpersonal relationships can improve teamwork and collaboration, leading to more effective project execution.
   - **Support Systems**: Personal connections can provide emotional support and help employees navigate workplace challenges.

2. **Increased Job Satisfaction**:
   - **Work Environment**: A supportive and friendly work environment contributes to higher job satisfaction and employee retention.
   - **Motivation**: Positive relationships with colleagues can increase motivation and engagement.

3. **Professional Growth**:
   - **Mentorship**: Intimate workplace relationships, such as mentorships, can facilitate professional development and career advancement.
   - **Networking**: Building personal connections can expand professional networks and open up new opportunities.

## Navigating Boundaries and Professionalism

1. **Setting Clear Boundaries**:
   - **Define Boundaries**: Clearly define the limits of personal and professional interactions to

maintain a professional atmosphere.

- ○ **Respect Privacy**: Respect colleagues' privacy and avoid overstepping personal boundaries.

2. **Maintaining Professionalism**:
   - ○ **Focus on Work**: Ensure that personal relationships do not interfere with work responsibilities and performance.
   - ○ **Avoid Favoritism**: Strive to treat all colleagues equally and avoid perceptions of favoritism or bias.

3. **Addressing Conflicts**:
   - ○ **Conflict Resolution**: Address conflicts promptly and professionally, focusing on resolving issues rather than personal grievances.
   - ○ **Seek Mediation**: If necessary, seek assistance from a manager or HR professional to mediate disputes.

4. **Handling Romantic Relationships**:
   - ○ **Company Policies**: Familiarize yourself with company policies regarding workplace romances and adhere to them.
   - ○ **Discretion**: Maintain discretion and professionalism in romantic relationships to avoid potential conflicts of interest or disruptions.

## Practical Strategies for Managing Workplace Intimacy

1. **Fostering Positive Relationships**:
   - ○ **Build Trust**: Develop trust by being reliable, supportive, and respectful towards colleagues.
   - ○ **Encourage Open Communication**: Promote

open and honest communication to strengthen relationships and address potential issues.

2. **Promoting Inclusivity**:
   - **Respect Differences**: Respect diverse perspectives and backgrounds, and foster an inclusive work environment.
   - **Encourage Team Activities**: Participate in team-building activities to enhance relationships and improve team dynamics.

3. **Balancing Personal and Professional Lives**:
   - **Set Personal Limits**: Establish limits on sharing personal information and avoid letting personal issues affect work performance.
   - **Maintain Work-Life Balance**: Ensure that personal relationships do not overshadow professional responsibilities.

4. **Managing Conflicts Effectively**:
   - **Address Issues Early**: Tackle any conflicts or concerns as soon as they arise to prevent escalation.
   - **Focus on Solutions**: Work towards solutions that address the root of the issue rather than assigning blame.

## Exercises for Enhancing Workplace Intimacy

1. **Team-Building Activities**:
   - **Organize Events**: Plan and participate in team-building events or social activities to strengthen relationships and improve collaboration.
   - **Feedback Sessions**: Conduct regular feedback sessions to discuss team dynamics

and areas for improvement.

2. **Communication Workshops**:
   - **Skill Development**: Attend workshops or training sessions to improve communication skills and learn effective conflict resolution techniques.
   - **Role-Playing**: Engage in role-playing exercises to practice handling various workplace scenarios and interactions.

3. **Mentorship Programs**:
   - **Establish Programs**: Participate in or establish mentorship programs to foster professional growth and build supportive relationships.
   - **Regular Check-Ins**: Schedule regular check-ins with mentors or mentees to discuss progress and address any concerns.

4. **Boundary Setting Exercise**:
   - **Create a Boundaries Checklist**: Develop a checklist of personal and professional boundaries to guide interactions with colleagues.
   - **Review and Reflect**: Regularly review and reflect on boundaries to ensure they are respected and maintained.

## Addressing Potential Pitfalls

1. **Navigating Gossip and Rumors**:
   - **Avoid Participation**: Refrain from participating in or spreading gossip and rumors that can damage relationships and workplace morale.
   - **Address Issues Directly**: Address any concerns or issues directly with the

individuals involved rather than discussing them with others.

2. **Managing Power Dynamics**:
   - **Be Aware of Hierarchies**: Be mindful of power dynamics and ensure that personal relationships do not influence professional decision-making.

   - **Maintain Professional Boundaries**: Maintain professionalism and avoid letting personal relationships affect work-related decisions.

3. **Preventing Burnout**:
   - **Balance Relationships**: Balance personal and professional relationships to prevent burnout and maintain job satisfaction.

   - **Seek Support**: If feeling overwhelmed, seek support from colleagues, mentors, or professional resources.

## Conclusion

Intimacy in the workplace can enhance job satisfaction, collaboration, and professional growth, but it must be navigated with care. By setting clear boundaries, maintaining professionalism, and fostering positive relationships, individuals can build meaningful connections while preserving a respectful and productive work environment. In the next chapter, we will explore the concept of resilience in relationships. We will discuss how resilience contributes to relationship stability and offer practical strategies for developing and maintaining resilience in intimate connections. Join us as we continue our exploration of intimacy and its impact on our lives.

# CHAPTER 38: BALANCING INTIMACY AND INDEPENDENCE

Striking a balance between intimacy and independence is essential for fostering healthy and fulfilling relationships. While intimacy involves emotional closeness and connection, independence refers to maintaining one's personal identity and autonomy. This chapter explores how individuals can nurture deep, meaningful relationships while preserving their individuality and sense of self.

**Understanding Intimacy and Independence**

1. **Definition and Scope**:
    - **Intimacy**: The emotional closeness and deep connection shared with another person, characterized by mutual trust, understanding, and support.
    - **Independence**: The ability to maintain one's own identity, make personal choices, and pursue individual goals and interests without undue reliance on others.

2. **Interconnection**:
    - **Complementary Roles**: Intimacy and independence are not mutually exclusive

but can complement each other. Healthy relationships involve both closeness and personal autonomy.

- **Potential Conflicts**: Balancing these aspects can sometimes be challenging, as intense intimacy might lead to dependency, while excessive independence might create emotional distance.

## Benefits of Balancing Intimacy and Independence

1. **Personal Growth**:
   - **Self-Discovery**: Maintaining independence allows individuals to explore their interests, values, and goals, contributing to personal growth and self-awareness.
   - **Enhanced Identity**: A strong sense of self fosters a more authentic and confident approach to intimacy, enriching relationships.

2. **Healthy Relationships**:
   - **Mutual Respect**: Balancing intimacy and independence fosters mutual respect and understanding, ensuring that both partners' needs and desires are honored.
   - **Reduced Dependency**: Independence helps prevent emotional dependency and allows for a more balanced, equitable relationship dynamic.

3. **Increased Relationship Satisfaction**:
   - **Fulfillment**: When individuals feel fulfilled and autonomous, they are more likely to contribute positively to their relationships and experience greater satisfaction.
   - **Resilience**: A balanced approach helps

relationships withstand challenges and changes, promoting resilience and stability.

**Strategies for Balancing Intimacy and Independence**

1. **Communicate Openly**:
   - **Express Needs and Boundaries**: Communicate your need for personal space and time, as well as your desire for connection, to your partner.
   - **Discuss Expectations**: Have open discussions about each other's expectations regarding intimacy and independence to align goals and avoid misunderstandings.

2. **Pursue Individual Interests**:
   - **Personal Hobbies**: Engage in activities and hobbies that you enjoy independently, contributing to a sense of fulfillment and self-growth.
   - **Professional Goals**: Focus on your career or personal ambitions to maintain a sense of purpose and achievement outside the relationship.

3. **Establish Boundaries**:
   - **Define Limits**: Set clear boundaries around personal time and space to ensure that both partners have opportunities for independence.
   - **Respect Boundaries**: Honor each other's boundaries and avoid encroaching on personal time or interests.

4. **Cultivate Mutual Support**:
   - **Encourage Growth**: Support each other's individual pursuits and celebrate personal achievements.

- **Offer Reassurance**: Provide emotional support and reassurance, affirming that independence does not diminish the value of the relationship.

5. **Foster Quality Time**:
   - **Plan Together**: Schedule quality time together to strengthen intimacy while ensuring that it complements rather than overshadows individual pursuits.
   - **Create Rituals**: Develop shared rituals or traditions that enhance connection and provide opportunities for bonding.

6. **Practice Self-Care**:
   - **Prioritize Well-being**: Engage in self-care practices that promote mental, emotional, and physical health, contributing to overall well-being and balance.
   - **Manage Stress**: Address and manage stress effectively to maintain a healthy equilibrium between personal and relational demands.

**Practical Exercises for Balancing Intimacy and Independence**

1. **Daily Check-Ins**:
   - **Routine**: Establish a daily or weekly check-in routine to discuss each other's needs, boundaries, and experiences.
   - **Feedback**: Use these check-ins to provide constructive feedback and address any concerns regarding intimacy and independence.

2. **Personal Goals Exercise**:
   - **Goal Setting**: Set personal and professional

goals that align with your values and interests. Share these goals with your partner to foster mutual support.

- **Progress Review**: Regularly review and discuss progress towards these goals to maintain motivation and accountability.

3. **Boundary Mapping**:
   - **Create a Map**: Develop a visual or written map of personal boundaries, including time, space, and emotional limits.
   - **Discuss and Adjust**: Review the map with your partner and make adjustments as needed to ensure that boundaries are respected and balanced.

4. **Quality Time Planning**:
   - **Plan Activities**: Plan regular activities or dates that allow for quality time together while also accommodating personal interests and commitments.
   - **Balance Scheduling**: Ensure that quality time is balanced with individual pursuits and responsibilities.

5. **Self-Care Routine**:
   - **Develop a Routine**: Create a self-care routine that includes activities that promote relaxation, enjoyment, and personal growth.
   - **Integrate Self-Care**: Integrate self-care into your daily or weekly schedule, ensuring that it complements your relationship and personal goals.

## Addressing Potential Challenges

1. **Navigating Jealousy or Insecurity**:

- ◦ **Open Dialogue**: Address any feelings of jealousy or insecurity through open and honest communication.
- ◦ **Reaffirm Commitment**: Reassure each other of your commitment to the relationship and discuss ways to manage concerns.

2. **Avoiding Overdependence**:
   - ◦ **Encourage Independence**: Foster independence by encouraging each other to pursue individual interests and maintain personal space.
   - ◦ **Set Limits**: Establish limits on how much time is spent together versus apart to prevent overdependence.

3. **Managing Conflicts**:
   - ◦ **Conflict Resolution**: Use effective conflict resolution techniques to address disagreements related to intimacy and independence.
   - ◦ **Seek Solutions**: Focus on finding mutually acceptable solutions that respect both partners' needs.

## Conclusion

Balancing intimacy and independence is crucial for maintaining healthy and fulfilling relationships. By communicating openly, pursuing individual interests, setting boundaries, and supporting each other, individuals can nurture deep connections while preserving their personal autonomy. In the next chapter, we will explore the concept of resilience in relationships. We will discuss how resilience contributes to relationship stability and offer practical strategies for developing and maintaining resilience in intimate connections. Join us as we continue our exploration of intimacy and its impact on our lives.

# CHAPTER 39: INTIMACY AND PERSONAL GROWTH

Personal growth and self-improvement are crucial components of enriching intimate relationships. By fostering self-awareness and emotional intelligence, individuals can contribute positively to their relationships and create deeper, more meaningful connections. This chapter explores the interplay between personal development and intimacy, offering practical tips for integrating growth into relational dynamics.

**Understanding Personal Growth and Intimacy**

1. **Definition and Scope**:
    - **Personal Growth**: The process of developing oneself through self-awareness, self-improvement, and the pursuit of personal goals. It includes enhancing skills, expanding knowledge, and evolving one's perspectives.
    - **Intimacy**: The emotional closeness and connection between individuals, characterized by trust, understanding, and mutual respect.

2. **Interconnection**:
    - **Mutual Enhancement**: Personal growth can enhance intimacy by increasing self-

awareness and emotional intelligence, leading to more fulfilling relationships. Conversely, intimate relationships can provide support and motivation for personal development.

- **Growth through Intimacy**: Engaging in intimate relationships can prompt individuals to reflect on their values, behaviors, and goals, fostering personal growth.

## Benefits of Integrating Personal Growth into Intimacy

1. **Increased Self-Awareness**:
   - **Understanding Self**: Personal growth fosters a deeper understanding of oneself, including one's needs, desires, and boundaries. This self-awareness enhances the ability to communicate effectively and build stronger connections.
   - **Emotional Regulation**: Improved emotional intelligence helps manage emotions and reactions, contributing to healthier and more balanced relationships.

2. **Enhanced Communication**:
   - **Effective Expression**: Personal development often includes learning how to express thoughts and feelings more clearly and constructively, which improves communication in intimate relationships.
   - **Active Listening**: Growth in self-awareness and empathy enhances active listening skills, fostering better understanding and connection with a partner.

3. **Strengthened Relationship Dynamics**:

- **Mutual Support**: Individuals who are committed to personal growth are often more supportive and encouraging of their partner's development, leading to a more collaborative and positive relationship dynamic.

- **Shared Goals**: Personal growth can align with relationship goals, creating a shared sense of purpose and direction.

4. **Greater Resilience**:

   - **Handling Challenges**: Personal growth equips individuals with the skills to handle relationship challenges and conflicts more effectively, contributing to resilience and stability in relationships.

   - **Adaptability**: Developing adaptability and coping strategies enhances the ability to navigate changes and difficulties within the relationship.

**Strategies for Integrating Personal Growth into Intimate Relationships**

1. **Cultivate Self-Awareness**:

   - **Reflect Regularly**: Engage in regular self-reflection to understand your values, motivations, and areas for improvement. Journaling or meditation can be useful tools for this practice.

   - **Seek Feedback**: Ask for constructive feedback from trusted friends, mentors, or therapists to gain insights into your behaviors and growth areas.

2. **Enhance Emotional Intelligence**:

   - **Practice Empathy**: Develop empathy by

actively trying to understand and share the feelings of others. This can improve emotional connection and support in relationships.

- **Manage Emotions**: Learn techniques for managing and regulating your emotions, such as mindfulness or stress reduction practices, to maintain emotional balance.

3. **Foster Open Communication**:
    - **Express Needs**: Communicate your needs and desires clearly and honestly with your partner, while also being open to hearing their perspectives.
    - **Active Listening**: Practice active listening skills by giving your full attention, reflecting on what your partner says, and responding thoughtfully.

4. **Support Each Other's Growth**:
    - **Encourage Development**: Support your partner's personal growth by encouraging their goals and aspirations. Celebrate their achievements and offer constructive support.
    - **Share Goals**: Discuss and align your personal and relationship goals to ensure that both partners are working towards shared objectives.

5. **Set and Pursue Personal Goals**:
    - **Define Objectives**: Identify personal growth goals, such as learning a new skill, pursuing education, or improving a specific area of your life.
    - **Track Progress**: Monitor your progress

towards these goals and adjust as needed, while sharing your journey with your partner.

6. **Embrace Vulnerability**:
   - **Share Growth Experiences**: Be open about your personal growth experiences and challenges with your partner. This vulnerability can deepen your emotional connection and understanding.
   - **Support Vulnerability**: Encourage and support your partner's vulnerability by creating a safe space for them to express their feelings and experiences.

**Practical Exercises for Integrating Personal Growth into Intimacy**

1. **Personal Growth Plan**:
   - **Create a Plan**: Develop a personal growth plan that outlines your goals, steps to achieve them, and strategies for overcoming obstacles.
   - **Review Regularly**: Schedule regular check-ins to review your progress and make adjustments as needed. Share this plan with your partner for support and accountability.

2. **Growth-Focused Conversations**:
   - **Weekly Discussions**: Set aside time each week for discussions focused on personal growth, including reflections, goals, and experiences.
   - **Growth Journals**: Maintain individual or joint growth journals where you record insights, achievements, and challenges related to personal development.

3. **Shared Learning Activities**:
    - **Attend Workshops**: Participate in workshops or seminars together that focus on personal growth topics, such as communication skills, emotional intelligence, or relationship dynamics.
    - **Read and Reflect**: Read books or articles on personal development and discuss key takeaways with your partner.

4. **Emotional Check-Ins**:
    - **Daily Check-Ins**: Incorporate brief daily emotional check-ins with your partner to discuss how you are feeling and any personal growth insights.
    - **Reflect Together**: Reflect on your individual and shared experiences, discussing how personal growth has impacted your relationship.

## Addressing Potential Challenges

1. **Balancing Growth and Relationship Needs**:
    - **Negotiate Priorities**: Discuss and negotiate how to balance personal growth activities with relationship needs to ensure that both areas are adequately addressed.
    - **Set Boundaries**: Establish boundaries to prevent personal growth pursuits from overshadowing relationship time and attention.

2. **Managing Expectations**:
    - **Align Goals**: Ensure that expectations for personal growth and relationship dynamics are aligned and mutually agreed upon.
    - **Communicate Changes**: Communicate any

changes in personal goals or growth plans to your partner to manage expectations and avoid misunderstandings.

3. **Handling Resistance**:
   - **Address Concerns**: Address any resistance or concerns from your partner regarding personal growth activities with open and honest communication.

   - **Seek Compromise**: Find compromises that accommodate both partners' needs and growth objectives, fostering a collaborative approach.

## Conclusion

Integrating personal growth into intimate relationships can enhance self-awareness, communication, and relationship satisfaction. By fostering self-awareness, enhancing emotional intelligence, and supporting each other's development, individuals can create more meaningful and fulfilling connections. In the next chapter, we will explore the role of resilience in relationships. We will discuss how resilience contributes to relationship stability and offer practical strategies for developing and maintaining resilience in intimate connections. Join us as we continue our exploration of intimacy and its impact on our lives.

# CHAPTER 40: INTIMACY IN CASUAL RELATIONSHIPS

Casual relationships are often characterized by their informal nature and lack of long-term commitment. Despite their transient or non-exclusive status, intimacy can still play a significant role. This chapter explores the nature of intimacy in casual relationships, providing insights into navigating boundaries, communication, and expectations to maintain a respectful and fulfilling connection.

**Understanding Intimacy in Casual Relationships**

1. **Definition and Scope**:
   - **Casual Relationships**: These are relationships where partners do not commit to a long-term future together. They can include dating, friends with benefits, or other informal connections.
   - **Intimacy**: In casual relationships, intimacy may include emotional, physical, or sexual closeness, but it is often more fluid and less defined than in committed relationships.

2. **Nature of Intimacy in Casual Relationships**:
   - **Variable Levels**: Intimacy in casual relationships can vary greatly based on individual preferences, the nature of the relationship, and mutual agreements.

- **Temporary Connections**: While the connection may be temporary or less formal, the experiences and interactions can still be deeply meaningful.

## Navigating Boundaries in Casual Relationships

1. **Establishing Boundaries**:
   - **Define Expectations**: Clearly define what each person wants and expects from the relationship. This includes discussing limits on emotional involvement, physical interactions, and future plans.
   - **Respect Privacy**: Maintain personal privacy and respect each other's space, avoiding the assumption that casual involvement warrants access to personal details or life events.

2. **Communicating Boundaries**:
   - **Open Dialogue**: Engage in open and honest conversations about boundaries and expectations. Ensure that both partners feel comfortable expressing their needs and limits.
   - **Regular Check-Ins**: Schedule regular check-ins to discuss how boundaries are being respected and to address any evolving concerns or changes in expectations.

3. **Handling Boundary Violations**:
   - **Address Issues Promptly**: If a boundary is crossed, address it promptly and calmly. Communicate how it affects you and discuss ways to prevent similar issues in the future.
   - **Re-evaluate the Relationship**: Consider whether the violation of boundaries affects

your desire to continue the relationship. Re-evaluate and adjust boundaries as necessary.

## Communication in Casual Relationships

1. **Importance of Clear Communication**:
   - **Express Needs and Desires**: Clearly communicate your needs, desires, and limitations to avoid misunderstandings and ensure that both partners are on the same page.
   - **Discuss Relationship Goals**: Talk about the goals and nature of the relationship to prevent assumptions and ensure alignment on what both partners want.

2. **Effective Communication Techniques**:
   - **Use "I" Statements**: Use "I" statements to express your feelings and needs without placing blame or making the other person feel defensive (e.g., "I feel uncomfortable when...").
   - **Active Listening**: Practice active listening by giving your full attention, reflecting on what the other person says, and responding thoughtfully.

3. **Managing Misunderstandings**:
   - **Clarify Misconceptions**: If misunderstandings arise, clarify them directly and openly. Seek to understand the other person's perspective and share your own.
   - **Avoid Assumptions**: Avoid making assumptions about the other person's feelings or intentions. Instead, ask

questions and seek clarity.

## Balancing Intimacy and Casual Nature

1. **Managing Emotional Involvement**:
   - **Stay True to Intentions**: Be mindful of the level of emotional involvement you are comfortable with and ensure it aligns with the casual nature of the relationship.
   - **Monitor Attachment**: Be aware of how your emotions might evolve and manage them to avoid becoming more invested than intended.

2. **Respecting Each Other's Space**:
   - **Maintain Independence**: Respect each other's need for personal space and independence, acknowledging that the casual nature of the relationship does not require constant interaction.
   - **Avoid Overdependence**: Prevent overdependence on the relationship for emotional support or validation.

3. **Navigating Change**:
   - **Discuss Changes Openly**: If either partner wants to change the nature of the relationship, discuss it openly and honestly. Evaluate how these changes align with both partners' needs and expectations.
   - **Be Prepared for Transition**: Be prepared for the possibility that the relationship may end or evolve, and handle transitions with respect and understanding.

## Enhancing Intimacy in Casual Relationships

1. **Creating Meaningful Connections**:
   - **Quality Time**: Spend quality time together

to build a meaningful connection, even if the relationship is casual. Engage in activities that foster enjoyment and bonding.

- **Express Appreciation**: Show appreciation and acknowledge positive aspects of the relationship. Small gestures of gratitude can enhance the connection and respect.

2. **Maintaining Respect and Integrity**:
   - **Honor Agreements**: Honor any agreements or boundaries set within the relationship, demonstrating respect for each other's needs and preferences.
   - **Practice Honesty**: Be honest about your intentions and feelings, avoiding deception or misrepresentation of the nature of the relationship.

3. **Fostering Mutual Understanding**:
   - **Share Perspectives**: Share your perspectives and listen to your partner's views on the relationship. Mutual understanding can strengthen the connection and improve the overall experience.
   - **Adapt Flexibly**: Be flexible and adaptable in your approach, recognizing that the dynamics of casual relationships may shift over time.

## Addressing Potential Challenges

1. **Dealing with Uncertainty**:
   - **Clarify Expectations**: Address any uncertainties or ambiguities by discussing expectations and goals openly. This can reduce anxiety and prevent

misunderstandings.

- ◦ **Communicate Regularly**: Maintain regular communication to address any emerging issues or changes in the relationship dynamic.

2. **Handling Differing Levels of Intimacy**:
   - ◦ **Discuss Differences**: If partners have differing levels of desire for intimacy, discuss these differences openly and seek common ground or understanding.
   - ◦ **Respect Choices**: Respect each other's choices and boundaries regarding intimacy, even if they differ from your own preferences.

3. **Navigating Emotional Complexity**:
   - ◦ **Manage Expectations**: Recognize and manage emotional complexities that may arise in a casual relationship, and adjust your expectations accordingly.
   - ◦ **Seek Support if Needed**: If emotional challenges become overwhelming, consider seeking support from a counselor or therapist to navigate these feelings.

## Conclusion

Intimacy in casual relationships can be complex, balancing informal dynamics with the need for clear communication and mutual respect. By establishing and maintaining boundaries, communicating effectively, and managing emotional involvement, individuals can create fulfilling and respectful connections. In the next chapter, we will explore the role of resilience in relationships, examining how resilience contributes to relationship stability and offering practical strategies for developing and maintaining resilience in intimate connections. Join us as we continue our exploration of intimacy and its impact on our lives.

# CHAPTER 41: THE ROLE OF PLAYFULNESS

Playfulness is often associated with light-hearted activities and spontaneous fun, but it also plays a crucial role in deepening intimacy. By fostering joy, creativity, and a sense of connection, playfulness can enhance relationships and strengthen bonds between individuals. This chapter explores the benefits of playfulness for intimacy and provides practical suggestions for incorporating play into relationships.

**Understanding the Role of Playfulness**

1. **Definition of Playfulness**:
    - **Playfulness**: Playfulness involves engaging in activities that are spontaneous, enjoyable, and often characterized by a sense of fun and creativity. It includes both physical and verbal interactions that encourage laughter, exploration, and shared enjoyment.

2. **Importance in Relationships**:
    - **Strengthening Bonds**: Playfulness helps to build and reinforce emotional connections, allowing partners to bond over shared experiences and laughter.

    - **Fostering Resilience**: Playful interactions can buffer against stress and conflicts, promoting resilience and a positive outlook within the relationship.

**Benefits of Playfulness for Intimacy**

1. **Enhancing Emotional Connection**:
   - **Building Trust**: Engaging in playful activities can foster trust and openness, creating a safe environment where individuals feel comfortable expressing themselves.
   - **Deepening Understanding**: Playfulness often leads to meaningful conversations and shared experiences, enhancing mutual understanding and empathy.

2. **Reducing Stress and Tension**:
   - **Easing Conflict**: Playful interactions can help diffuse tension and ease conflicts, making it easier to address and resolve issues in a relaxed and constructive manner.
   - **Promoting Relaxation**: Laughter and playfulness promote relaxation and well-being, reducing stress and contributing to a more positive relationship environment.

3. **Encouraging Creativity**:
   - **Exploring New Dimensions**: Playfulness encourages individuals to explore new dimensions of their relationship, fostering creativity and innovation in how they connect and interact.
   - **Breaking Routine**: Engaging in playful activities helps break routine and monotony, injecting freshness and excitement into the relationship.

4. **Strengthening Bonding**:
   - **Shared Joy**: Experiencing joy and fun

together strengthens the emotional bond between individuals, creating lasting memories and reinforcing the connection.

- **Mutual Enjoyment**: Playful interactions provide opportunities for mutual enjoyment and shared laughter, enhancing the overall satisfaction in the relationship.

**Incorporating Playfulness into Relationships**

1. **Engaging in Fun Activities**:
   - **Try New Hobbies**: Explore new hobbies or activities together that spark interest and excitement. This could include sports, games, or creative projects.
   - **Plan Spontaneous Outings**: Surprise each other with spontaneous outings or activities that break the routine and offer opportunities for shared fun.

2. **Fostering a Playful Attitude**:
   - **Be Open to Play**: Approach interactions with a playful attitude, embracing opportunities for humor, laughter, and light-heartedness.
   - **Encourage Creativity**: Encourage each other to be creative and imaginative, exploring new ways to connect and have fun.

3. **Using Humor**:
   - **Share Jokes**: Share jokes, funny stories, or humorous observations to bring laughter and joy into your interactions.
   - **Laugh Together**: Find reasons to laugh together, whether through movies, comedy shows, or playful banter.

4. **Playing Games**:
   - **Board Games and Puzzles**: Engage in board

games, puzzles, or other interactive games that promote collaboration and enjoyment.

- **Outdoor Activities**: Participate in outdoor games or sports that provide opportunities for physical activity and fun.

5. **Creating Rituals**:
   - **Daily Playfulness**: Incorporate playful rituals into your daily routine, such as playful greetings, shared jokes, or small acts of fun.
   - **Special Traditions**: Develop special traditions or rituals that include playful elements, such as themed date nights or creative celebrations.

## Addressing Challenges

1. **Balancing Playfulness and Seriousness**:
   - **Recognize Boundaries**: Understand and respect each other's boundaries and comfort levels regarding playfulness, balancing it with the need for seriousness and respect.
   - **Adapt Playfulness**: Adapt playful interactions to fit the context of the relationship and individual preferences, ensuring that playfulness enhances rather than detracts from the connection.

2. **Navigating Different Preferences**:
   - **Communicate Preferences**: Discuss and understand each other's preferences for playfulness and find common ground that works for both partners.
   - **Be Flexible**: Be open to experimenting with different forms of play and adjusting based on feedback and mutual enjoyment.

3. **Addressing Resistance to Playfulness**:
   - **Understand Resistance**: If one partner is resistant to playfulness, explore the reasons behind it and address any concerns or discomfort they may have.
   - **Gradual Introduction**: Introduce playful activities gradually and gently, allowing the partner to become more comfortable with the idea over time.

## Examples of Playful Activities

1. **Playful Challenges**:
   - **Friendly Competitions**: Engage in friendly competitions or challenges, such as cooking contests, trivia games, or sports matches.
   - **Creative Projects**: Work on creative projects together, such as crafting, painting, or building something fun and imaginative.

2. **Playful Conversations**:
   - **Role-Playing**: Engage in light-hearted role-playing or create imaginary scenarios to explore and enjoy together.
   - **Whimsical Questions**: Ask whimsical or playful questions to spark interesting and entertaining conversations.

3. **Playful Surprises**:
   - **Surprise Dates**: Plan surprise dates or activities that include playful elements, such as scavenger hunts or themed adventures.
   - **Random Acts of Fun**: Surprise your partner with random acts of fun, such as leaving a funny note or planning an unexpected outing.

## Conclusion

Playfulness is a powerful tool for enhancing intimacy, bringing joy, spontaneity, and connection to relationships. By incorporating playful activities, fostering a playful attitude, and addressing challenges, individuals can strengthen their bonds and create a more fulfilling and enjoyable relationship. In the next chapter, we will explore the role of commitment in relationships, examining how commitment influences intimacy and offering strategies for cultivating and maintaining a strong commitment. Join us as we continue our exploration of intimacy and its impact on our lives.

# CHAPTER 42: INTIMACY IN ADVERSITY

Adversity often tests the strength and resilience of intimate relationships. While challenging times can strain connections, they also present opportunities to deepen bonds through shared experiences and mutual support. This chapter explores how to maintain and enhance intimacy during difficult periods, focusing on the role of support, understanding, and resilience in strengthening relationships.

**Understanding Intimacy in Adversity**

1. **Definition of Adversity**:
   - **Adversity**: Adversity refers to challenging or difficult situations that individuals may face, such as health issues, financial problems, loss, or major life changes. These situations can create stress and strain in relationships but also provide opportunities for growth and deepened connection.

2. **Impact on Intimacy**:
   - **Challenges to Connection**: Adversity can create emotional and physical barriers that challenge intimacy, making it harder to maintain closeness and connection.

   - **Opportunities for Growth**: Despite the difficulties, facing adversity together can strengthen relationships by fostering resilience, empathy, and a deeper understanding of each other.

## The Role of Support in Adversity

1. **Providing Emotional Support**:
   - **Active Listening**: Offer a listening ear without judgment, allowing your partner to express their feelings and concerns openly.
   - **Validation**: Validate your partner's emotions and experiences, showing empathy and understanding even when you may not fully comprehend their situation.

2. **Offering Practical Assistance**:
   - **Help with Tasks**: Provide practical support by helping with daily tasks or responsibilities that may become overwhelming during challenging times.
   - **Resource Sharing**: Share resources or seek out additional support services that can assist in managing the adversity.

3. **Encouraging Resilience**:
   - **Positive Reinforcement**: Encourage and reinforce each other's strengths and resilience, acknowledging efforts and progress in overcoming difficulties.
   - **Shared Goals**: Work together to set and achieve small goals that contribute to managing the adversity and rebuilding stability.

## Maintaining Communication During Difficult Times

1. **Open Dialogue**:
   - **Express Needs and Feelings**: Communicate openly about your own needs and feelings,

and encourage your partner to do the same.

- **Regular Check-Ins**: Schedule regular check-ins to discuss how each person is coping with the adversity and to address any emerging issues.

2. **Navigating Conflict**:
   - **Address Conflicts Constructively**: Approach conflicts with a focus on resolution rather than blame, using constructive communication techniques.
   - **Seek Compromise**: Be willing to find compromise and collaborate on solutions that address both partners' needs and concerns.

3. **Maintaining Connection**:
   - **Quality Time**: Make time for each other amidst the challenges, engaging in activities that provide comfort and connection.
   - **Affection and Reassurance**: Offer physical affection and verbal reassurance to strengthen the emotional bond and provide a sense of security.

**Building Resilience Together**

1. **Developing Shared Coping Strategies**:
   - **Joint Problem-Solving**: Work together to develop strategies for managing and overcoming adversity, focusing on collaborative problem-solving.
   - **Mutual Support Networks**: Build or strengthen support networks that can offer additional assistance and encouragement.

2. **Fostering Empathy and Understanding**:
   - **Perspective-Taking**: Make an effort to

understand your partner's perspective and experience, showing empathy and compassion for their situation.

- **Shared Experiences**: Share experiences and reflections related to the adversity, fostering a sense of solidarity and mutual understanding.

3. **Celebrating Small Victories**:
   - **Acknowledge Achievements**: Recognize and celebrate small victories and milestones achieved during the adversity, reinforcing positive progress and resilience.

   - **Express Gratitude**: Express gratitude for each other's support and efforts, strengthening the sense of partnership and appreciation.

## Addressing Common Challenges

1. **Managing Stress and Tension**:
   - **Stress Reduction Techniques**: Use stress reduction techniques such as mindfulness, relaxation exercises, or physical activity to manage stress and maintain emotional balance.

   - **Seek Professional Help**: Consider seeking professional help, such as counseling or therapy, to address any significant stress or relational issues arising from the adversity.

2. **Balancing Individual and Shared Needs**:
   - **Self-Care**: Ensure that both partners are taking care of their individual needs and well-being, as this contributes to overall relationship health.

   - **Shared Responsibility**: Balance the

responsibility for managing adversity between partners, avoiding the burden falling disproportionately on one person.

3. **Maintaining Hope and Optimism**:
   - **Focus on Positives**: Focus on positive aspects and potential opportunities for growth despite the challenges, maintaining a hopeful outlook on the future.

   - **Encourage Optimism**: Support each other in cultivating an optimistic perspective, reinforcing confidence in overcoming the adversity together.

## Practical Strategies for Nurturing Intimacy in Adversity

1. **Create Rituals of Connection**:
   - **Daily Check-Ins**: Establish daily or weekly rituals for checking in with each other, discussing feelings and experiences related to the adversity.

   - **Comforting Traditions**: Develop comforting traditions or rituals that provide solace and strengthen the bond during difficult times.

2. **Engage in Joint Activities**:
   - **Shared Projects**: Engage in joint projects or activities that provide a sense of purpose and achievement, helping to foster connection and collaboration.

   - **Enjoyable Experiences**: Prioritize enjoyable experiences that offer relief and pleasure, helping to maintain a positive connection amidst the challenges.

3. **Practice Forgiveness and Patience**:
   - **Forgive Mistakes**: Practice forgiveness

and understanding when mistakes or frustrations arise, recognizing that adversity can heighten emotional responses.

- **Be Patient**: Exercise patience with each other as you navigate the adversity, acknowledging that both partners may need time and support to cope effectively.

## Conclusion

Adversity presents both challenges and opportunities for intimate relationships. By focusing on support, communication, and resilience, partners can strengthen their bond and deepen their connection even in the face of difficulties. Maintaining intimacy during challenging times requires effort, empathy, and mutual understanding, but it can lead to a more resilient and fulfilling relationship. In the next chapter, we will explore the impact of personal growth on intimacy, examining how self-improvement can enhance relational connections and offer practical strategies for integrating personal development into relationships. Join us as we continue our exploration of intimacy and its transformative power.

# CHAPTER 43: THE FUTURE OF INTIMACY

As society evolves, so do the dynamics of intimacy. The way we form, maintain, and experience intimate relationships is influenced by technological advancements, social changes, and cultural shifts. This chapter explores emerging trends and potential future developments in intimate relationships, offering insights into how intimacy may evolve in the coming years.

**Technological Advances and Their Impact**

1. **Virtual and Augmented Reality**:
    - **Enhanced Communication**: Virtual and augmented reality technologies are creating new ways for people to connect and interact. These technologies offer immersive experiences that could transform how people experience intimacy, enabling virtual presence and interaction in ways that were previously impossible.

    - **Emotional Connection**: VR and AR can enhance emotional connection by providing immersive environments for shared experiences, such as virtual dates or interactive social spaces, making it easier to maintain relationships across distances.

2. **Artificial Intelligence and Relationship Management**:

- **AI Companions**: AI-powered companions and chatbots are becoming more sophisticated, potentially offering emotional support and companionship. While these technologies can provide some level of interaction, they may also raise questions about the nature and authenticity of emotional connections.

- **Personalized Insights**: AI can analyze relationship patterns and provide personalized advice or interventions to improve communication and intimacy, helping individuals and couples navigate their relationships more effectively.

3. **Wearable Technology**:
   - **Biofeedback**: Wearable devices that monitor physiological responses, such as heart rate or stress levels, can provide insights into emotional states and relational dynamics. This technology may help individuals understand and manage their emotional experiences, potentially enhancing intimacy.

   - **Shared Health Data**: Wearables that share health data between partners could foster greater understanding and support, allowing individuals to be more attuned to each other's well-being.

**Social and Cultural Shifts**

1. **Changing Relationship Norms**:
   - **Non-Traditional Relationships**: There is growing acceptance of non-traditional relationship structures, such as polyamory, open relationships, and cohabitation

without marriage. These evolving norms reflect changing attitudes toward intimacy and may lead to more diverse and inclusive relationship practices.

- **Redefining Commitment**: The concept of commitment is evolving, with some individuals seeking new ways to define and express their commitment in relationships. This shift may influence how intimacy is experienced and understood.

2. **Increased Focus on Mental Health**:
    - **Therapeutic Approaches**: As mental health awareness grows, there is increasing emphasis on therapeutic approaches to enhance relationship health and intimacy. Couples therapy, individual counseling, and mental health support are becoming integral to maintaining and improving intimate connections.

    - **Self-Care and Well-Being**: The focus on self-care and personal well-being is shaping how individuals approach intimacy. Prioritizing mental health and self-awareness can lead to healthier, more fulfilling relationships.

3. **Cultural Diversity and Globalization**:
    - **Cross-Cultural Relationships**: Globalization and cultural exchange are bringing together individuals from diverse backgrounds, leading to the development of cross-cultural relationships. These relationships can enrich experiences of intimacy but may also require navigating cultural differences and expectations.

    - **Cultural Sensitivity**: Increasing cultural

sensitivity and awareness may lead to more inclusive and respectful approaches to intimacy, acknowledging and valuing diverse perspectives and practices.

## Ethical Considerations and Challenges

1. **Privacy and Security**:
   - **Data Privacy**: As technology becomes more integrated into intimate relationships, concerns about data privacy and security are becoming more prominent. Individuals must navigate how their personal information is collected, used, and protected.
   - **Consent and Autonomy**: Ensuring that technology respects personal consent and autonomy is crucial. Ethical considerations regarding the use of AI, wearables, and other technologies in relationships must be addressed to maintain trust and respect.

2. **Authenticity and Connection**:
   - **Virtual vs. Real Connection**: The rise of virtual and AI-driven interactions raises questions about the authenticity of connections. Balancing virtual experiences with genuine, face-to-face interactions is essential to maintain meaningful intimacy.
   - **Human Touch**: Despite technological advancements, the need for physical and emotional human touch remains fundamental. Ensuring that technology complements rather than replaces human connection is vital for preserving intimacy.

## Preparing for the Future of Intimacy

1. **Embracing Change**:
   - **Adaptability**: Embracing technological and social changes while maintaining core principles of intimacy, such as trust, empathy, and communication, will be essential for navigating the future of relationships.
   - **Continuous Learning**: Staying informed about emerging trends and developments in intimacy can help individuals and couples adapt and thrive in evolving relational landscapes.
2. **Cultivating Connection**:
   - **Fostering Genuine Interactions**: Prioritizing authentic, meaningful interactions in both digital and physical spaces will help preserve the depth and richness of intimate relationships.
   - **Balancing Technology and Human Experience**: Striking a balance between technological innovations and human experiences will be key to maintaining and enhancing intimacy in the future.

## Conclusion

The future of intimacy is shaped by technological advances, social changes, and cultural shifts. While these developments present new opportunities for connection and interaction, they also raise important ethical and practical considerations. By embracing change, fostering genuine connections, and balancing technology with human experience, individuals and couples can navigate the evolving landscape of intimacy and build fulfilling, resilient relationships. In the next chapter, we will explore strategies for fostering lifelong intimacy, offering practical advice and insights for sustaining deep connections over time. Join us as we continue our journey into the multifaceted world of intimacy.

# CHAPTER 44: NURTURING INTIMACY IN DAILY LIFE

Intimacy is not just a grand gesture or a special occasion; it is nurtured through the consistency of daily interactions and experiences. Building and maintaining intimacy involves making a conscious effort to connect with your partner, friends, or loved ones in meaningful ways. This chapter offers practical tips for nurturing intimacy in daily life, emphasizing the importance of small gestures, quality time, and consistent communication.

**Small Gestures of Affection**

1. **Express Appreciation**:
    - **Daily Compliments**: Regularly offering sincere compliments and acknowledging the qualities you admire in your partner or loved ones can strengthen your bond. Simple remarks such as, "I appreciate how thoughtful you are," or "You look great today," help reinforce your affection and appreciation.

    - **Gratitude Notes**: Leaving small notes of gratitude or appreciation in unexpected places, such as in a lunchbox or on a pillow, can create moments of joy and remind your loved ones of your care and attention.

2. **Acts of Kindness**:
   - **Small Surprises**: Thoughtful surprises, like bringing home their favorite snack or planning a spontaneous outing, show that you are thinking of them and value their happiness. These actions don't need to be elaborate; often, it's the little things that matter most.

   - **Helpful Gestures**: Offering to help with daily tasks, such as running an errand or taking care of chores, can demonstrate your support and commitment. Acts of service can be powerful ways to show that you are invested in your relationship.

3. **Physical Touch**:
   - **Affectionate Touch**: Regular physical touch, such as holding hands, hugging, or a gentle touch on the shoulder, can reinforce emotional connection and intimacy. These small gestures create a sense of closeness and warmth.

   - **Affectionate Rituals**: Developing routines that include physical affection, such as a morning hug or an evening cuddle, can help maintain a consistent level of intimacy in your daily life.

## Quality Time Together

1. **Intentional Time**:
   - **Scheduled Moments**: Set aside specific times for each other, free from distractions. Whether it's a weekly date night, a daily meal together, or a dedicated hour for

conversation, intentional time helps you stay connected and engaged.

- **Shared Activities**: Engage in activities you both enjoy, such as cooking together, exercising, or pursuing a common hobby. Shared experiences foster a sense of togetherness and create opportunities for bonding.

2. **Meaningful Conversations**:
   - **Deep Discussions**: Make time for meaningful conversations where you can discuss your feelings, dreams, and experiences. Avoid surface-level topics and focus on topics that encourage deeper understanding and emotional connection.
   - **Active Listening**: Practice active listening by giving your full attention, showing empathy, and responding thoughtfully. Listening attentively helps build trust and shows that you value the other person's perspective.

3. **Quality Over Quantity**:
   - **Focused Attention**: When spending time together, prioritize quality over quantity. Ensure that your interactions are present and meaningful, rather than just filling time. Focus on being fully engaged and connected during your shared moments.

## Consistent Communication

1. **Open Dialogue**:
   - **Express Feelings**: Regularly share your thoughts, feelings, and experiences with each other. Open and honest communication helps build trust and

intimacy by allowing both parties to understand and support each other's needs.

- **Address Issues Promptly**: Address any concerns or issues as they arise, rather than letting them fester. Early communication about problems can prevent misunderstandings and strengthen your relationship.

2. **Affectionate Communication**:
   - **Express Love**: Regularly express your love and appreciation through verbal affirmations. Simple phrases like "I love you," "I'm grateful for you," or "You mean a lot to me," can reinforce your emotional connection.
   - **Share Positives**: Make it a habit to share positive feedback and affirmations. Complimenting your partner, acknowledging their efforts, and celebrating their achievements can enhance your emotional bond.

3. **Routine Check-Ins**:
   - **Emotional Check-Ins**: Schedule regular check-ins to discuss how you are feeling and how the relationship is progressing. These check-ins provide an opportunity to address any concerns, share your experiences, and ensure that both partners feel heard and valued.
   - **Relationship Goals**: Discuss and set relationship goals together, whether they are related to personal growth, shared experiences, or future plans. Setting goals helps create a sense of shared purpose and

direction in your relationship.

## Balancing Individual and Shared Needs

1. **Respecting Independence**:
   - **Personal Space**: Respect each other's need for personal space and independence. Allowing time for individual interests and activities ensures that both partners feel fulfilled and valued in their own right.
   - **Support Individual Goals**: Encourage and support each other's personal goals and aspirations. Showing interest and providing encouragement for individual pursuits strengthens the overall dynamic of the relationship.

2. **Balancing Togetherness**:
   - **Shared Experiences**: While respecting personal space, also make time for shared experiences that strengthen your bond. Balancing individual needs with shared activities creates a harmonious relationship dynamic.
   - **Mutual Support**: Offer support and understanding for each other's needs and aspirations. Strive to find a balance between nurturing your relationship and supporting personal growth.

## Conclusion

Nurturing intimacy in daily life involves consistent effort and attention to the small, everyday moments that build connection and understanding. By focusing on small gestures of affection, quality time, consistent communication, and balancing individual and shared needs, you can strengthen your relationships and create a deeper, more meaningful bond. Intimacy is cultivated through the everyday practices of care, attention, and mutual respect, ensuring that your relationships remain vibrant and fulfilling over time. As we continue exploring the multifaceted aspects of intimacy, the next chapter will delve into practical strategies for maintaining intimacy in the long term, offering insights and guidance for sustaining deep connections throughout life's journey.

# CHAPTER 45: THE IMPACT OF TRAUMA ON INTIMACY

Trauma can profoundly affect an individual's ability to form and maintain intimate relationships. The emotional and psychological wounds from traumatic experiences can create barriers to trust, communication, and connection. This chapter explores how trauma influences intimacy and offers strategies for healing and rebuilding trust.

**Understanding Trauma and Its Effects**

1. **Defining Trauma**:
    - **Types of Trauma**: Trauma can result from various experiences, including abuse, neglect, loss, or significant life events. It can be acute (one-time events) or chronic (repeated or prolonged exposure).

    - **Trauma Responses**: Individuals may respond to trauma in different ways, including through emotional distress, avoidance, or hypervigilance. Understanding these responses is crucial for addressing their impact on intimacy.

2. **Effects of Trauma on Intimacy**:
    - **Trust Issues**: Trauma often leads to difficulties in trusting others. Individuals may fear betrayal or rejection, making it

challenging to open up and connect deeply with others.

- **Emotional Regulation**: Trauma can affect emotional regulation, leading to mood swings, anxiety, or emotional numbness. These difficulties can interfere with the ability to engage in healthy, stable relationships.

- **Communication Barriers**: Trauma can create barriers to effective communication, such as avoidance, difficulty expressing feelings, or fear of conflict. These barriers can hinder the development of intimacy.

**Healing from Trauma**

1. **Seeking Professional Help**:

    - **Therapy**: Professional therapy, such as cognitive-behavioral therapy (CBT), trauma-focused therapy, or EMDR (Eye Movement Desensitization and Reprocessing), can help individuals process and heal from trauma. Therapists provide tools and strategies for managing trauma responses and rebuilding trust.

    - **Support Groups**: Joining support groups with others who have experienced similar traumas can provide a sense of community and understanding. Sharing experiences and receiving support can aid in the healing process.

2. **Self-Care and Emotional Processing**:

    - **Mindfulness and Relaxation**: Practices such as mindfulness, meditation, and relaxation techniques can help individuals manage stress and emotional responses related to trauma. These practices promote self-awareness and emotional stability.

- **Journaling**: Writing about feelings and experiences can be a therapeutic way to process emotions and gain insight into trauma-related challenges. Journaling can also help individuals track their progress in healing.

3. **Building Resilience**:
- **Developing Coping Skills**: Learning and practicing coping skills, such as emotional regulation techniques and stress management strategies, can help individuals navigate the impact of trauma on their relationships.

- **Fostering Self-Compassion**: Cultivating self-compassion and understanding that healing is a gradual process can help individuals be patient with themselves and their progress.

## Rebuilding Trust and Intimacy

1. **Open Communication**:
- **Discussing Trauma**: When appropriate, sharing one's experience of trauma with a partner can foster understanding and empathy. Open communication about trauma can help build a foundation of trust and support.

- **Setting Boundaries**: Establishing and respecting personal boundaries is essential for creating a safe space in relationships. Clearly communicating boundaries helps prevent re-traumatization and supports healthy interactions.

2. **Gradual Exposure**:
    - **Taking Small Steps**: Rebuilding intimacy may involve taking gradual steps toward connection and vulnerability. Small, incremental efforts to engage in intimate interactions can help individuals build confidence and comfort over time.
    - **Building Safe Spaces**: Creating environments where individuals feel safe and supported can facilitate healing and trust-building. Safe spaces encourage open communication and emotional exploration.

3. **Mutual Support**:
    - **Partner Support**: Partners can play a crucial role in the healing process by offering patience, understanding, and encouragement. Providing emotional support and acknowledging the impact of trauma can strengthen the relationship.
    - **Shared Healing Journey**: Engaging in joint activities, such as therapy or self-care practices, can help couples work together to address trauma-related challenges and foster intimacy.

## Addressing Common Challenges

1. **Fear of Vulnerability**:
    - **Overcoming Fear**: Trauma can lead to a fear of vulnerability and rejection. Gradually building trust through consistent, supportive interactions can help individuals feel safer in expressing their emotions and needs.
    - **Reinforcing Trust**: Consistently demonstrating reliability and support helps

reinforce trust and reduces fear. Small, positive experiences of connection can build confidence in the relationship.

2. **Managing Triggers**:
    - **Identifying Triggers**: Recognizing and understanding trauma triggers is essential for managing their impact on intimacy. Partners can work together to identify and address triggers, creating strategies to navigate them constructively.

    - **Developing Coping Strategies**: Implementing coping strategies, such as grounding techniques or communication plans, can help manage triggers and prevent them from undermining the relationship.

3. **Balancing Healing and Relationship Growth**:
    - **Managing Expectations**: Healing from trauma is a dynamic process that can affect relationship growth. Partners should communicate openly about their expectations and adjust them as needed to accommodate the healing journey.

    - **Celebrating Progress**: Recognizing and celebrating progress, no matter how small, can provide motivation and reinforce positive changes in the relationship. Acknowledging achievements fosters a sense of accomplishment and hope.

## Conclusion

Trauma can significantly impact an individual's ability to develop and maintain intimate relationships, influencing trust, communication, and emotional regulation. By seeking professional help, practicing self-care, and employing strategies to rebuild trust, individuals can work towards healing and strengthening their relationships. Open communication, mutual support, and addressing common challenges are essential for navigating the effects of trauma and fostering deeper, more meaningful connections. In the next chapter, we will explore practical strategies for maintaining intimacy in long-term relationships, focusing on sustaining deep connections over time and navigating the evolving dynamics of enduring partnerships.

# CHAPTER 46: HEALING AND REBUILDING INTIMACY

Healing from past wounds is crucial for cultivating and sustaining meaningful, intimate relationships. Whether the wounds are from previous relationships, trauma, or personal challenges, addressing these issues is fundamental to developing healthier connections with others. This chapter explores the process of healing and offers guidance on rebuilding intimacy to foster deeper, more fulfilling relationships.

**Understanding the Need for Healing**

1. **Recognizing the Impact of Past Wounds**:
   - **Types of Wounds**: Past wounds can include emotional scars from previous relationships, unresolved trauma, or personal insecurities. These wounds can create barriers to intimacy, affecting trust, communication, and emotional openness.
   - **Impact on Relationships**: Unaddressed wounds can lead to patterns of behavior that hinder intimacy, such as avoidance, mistrust, or defensiveness. Understanding the impact of these wounds is essential for

addressing them effectively.

2. **The Healing Process**:
   - **Acknowledgment and Acceptance**: Healing begins with acknowledging and accepting past wounds. Denial or avoidance can prevent progress, so recognizing and validating these experiences is the first step towards healing.

   - **Emotional Processing**: Processing emotions related to past wounds involves exploring and understanding the feelings associated with them. This may include sadness, anger, guilt, or fear. Emotional processing helps individuals gain insight and work through these feelings.

**Strategies for Healing**

1. **Seeking Professional Support**:
   - **Therapy**: Professional therapy can provide valuable tools and support for healing from past wounds. Therapeutic approaches, such as cognitive-behavioral therapy (CBT), trauma-focused therapy, or psychodynamic therapy, can help individuals address underlying issues and develop healthier relational patterns.

   - **Counseling**: Relationship counseling or couples therapy can be beneficial for addressing issues that impact intimacy in partnerships. Counselors can help partners navigate challenges, improve communication, and rebuild trust.

2. **Practicing Self-Care**:
   - **Self-Compassion**: Practicing self-compassion involves treating oneself with

kindness and understanding. This approach helps individuals cope with their wounds without self-judgment, fostering a positive self-image and emotional resilience.

- **Self-Reflection**: Engaging in self-reflection through journaling, meditation, or other introspective practices can aid in understanding personal triggers and patterns. Self-reflection promotes insight and growth.

3. **Building Emotional Resilience**:
   - **Developing Coping Skills**: Learning and practicing coping skills, such as mindfulness, stress management, and emotional regulation techniques, can enhance emotional resilience. These skills help individuals navigate challenges and maintain stability in relationships.
   - **Setting Healthy Boundaries**: Establishing and maintaining healthy boundaries is crucial for protecting oneself from re-traumatization and fostering a safe space for intimacy. Clear boundaries promote mutual respect and understanding.

## Rebuilding Intimacy

1. **Fostering Open Communication**:
   - **Honest Dialogue**: Engaging in honest and open dialogue about past wounds and current needs is essential for rebuilding intimacy. Clear communication helps partners understand each other's experiences and expectations.
   - **Active Listening**: Practicing active listening involves giving full attention to the speaker,

validating their feelings, and responding empathetically. Active listening enhances connection and trust.

2. **Cultivating Trust**:
   - **Consistency and Reliability**: Rebuilding trust requires consistency and reliability in actions and communication. Demonstrating reliability over time helps partners feel secure and supported.
   - **Forgiveness and Reconciliation**: Addressing past hurts and working towards forgiveness can help repair relationships. Reconciliation involves acknowledging mistakes, making amends, and committing to positive changes.

3. **Nurturing Emotional Connection**:
   - **Quality Time**: Spending quality time together fosters emotional connection and intimacy. Engaging in shared activities and creating meaningful experiences can strengthen the bond between partners.
   - **Expressing Appreciation**: Regularly expressing appreciation and gratitude for one another reinforces positive feelings and deepens emotional connection. Simple acts of kindness and acknowledgment can have a significant impact.

## Addressing Common Challenges

1. **Managing Expectations**:
   - **Setting Realistic Goals**: Rebuilding intimacy takes time and effort. Setting realistic goals and expectations helps manage the process and prevents frustration. Recognizing that progress may

be gradual can help maintain motivation.

- **Avoiding Perfectionism**: Embracing imperfection and acknowledging that relationships have ups and downs can reduce pressure and promote a healthier perspective on intimacy.

2. **Navigating Relational Patterns**:

- **Identifying Patterns**: Recognizing and addressing recurring relational patterns, such as conflict styles or communication issues, can help prevent setbacks. Understanding these patterns allows individuals to work towards positive change.

- **Creating Positive Change**: Implementing new strategies for communication, conflict resolution, and emotional support can foster a healthier dynamic. Positive changes contribute to rebuilding and strengthening intimacy.

## Maintaining Healthy Intimacy

1. **Continuous Growth**:

- **Ongoing Self-Improvement**: Personal growth and self-improvement are ongoing processes. Continuously working on emotional resilience, communication skills, and self-awareness supports the maintenance of healthy intimacy.

- **Adapting to Change**: Relationships evolve over time, and adapting to changes in life circumstances or personal growth is essential for sustaining intimacy. Flexibility and adaptability promote long-term connection.

2. **Celebrating Milestones**:
   - **Acknowledging Progress**: Celebrating milestones and achievements in the healing process helps reinforce positive change and build confidence. Recognizing progress fosters a sense of accomplishment and hope.

   - **Fostering Positivity**: Maintaining a positive outlook and focusing on the strengths of the relationship can enhance intimacy. Emphasizing positive aspects and shared goals supports a healthy, fulfilling connection.

## Conclusion

Healing and rebuilding intimacy from past wounds involves a multifaceted approach, including seeking professional support, practicing self-care, and fostering open communication. By addressing underlying issues, cultivating trust, and nurturing emotional connection, individuals and couples can create healthier, more fulfilling relationships. Navigating common challenges and focusing on continuous growth and celebration of progress can help maintain and strengthen intimacy over time. In the next chapter, we will explore strategies for sustaining intimacy in long-term relationships, focusing on the dynamics of enduring partnerships and the evolution of connection over time.

# CHAPTER 47: INTIMACY AND ETHICAL NON-MONOGAMY

Ethical non-monogamy (ENM) encompasses various relationship structures where individuals engage in consensual and transparent relationships with multiple partners. This chapter explores the dynamics of intimacy within non-monogamous relationships, emphasizing the critical role of communication, trust, and mutual understanding. By examining the unique aspects of ENM, we aim to provide insights into fostering intimacy while navigating the complexities of multiple-partner relationships.

**Understanding Ethical Non-Monogamy**

1. **Defining Ethical Non-Monogamy**:
   - **Concept and Variants**: Ethical non-monogamy refers to relationship styles that involve consensual engagement with more than one partner. Variants include polyamory, open relationships, swinging, and relationship anarchy. Each style has its own set of principles and practices.

   - **Key Principles**: The foundational principles of ENM include consent, transparency, and mutual respect. All parties involved are aware of and agree to the nature of the relationships, and there is an emphasis on ethical behavior and open communication.

2. **Challenges and Misconceptions**:
   - **Common Misconceptions**: ENM is often misunderstood as inherently unstable or unethical. Misconceptions include assumptions about infidelity, lack of commitment, or inherent jealousy. Understanding the nuances of ENM can dispel these myths and provide a clearer perspective.

   - **Navigating Challenges**: ENM relationships can face unique challenges, such as managing jealousy, balancing time among multiple partners, and addressing societal stigma. Recognizing and addressing these challenges is crucial for maintaining healthy and intimate relationships.

## Building Intimacy in Non-Monogamous Relationships

1. **Establishing Clear Communication**:
   - **Honest Dialogue**: Clear and honest communication is essential in ENM. Partners must discuss their needs, boundaries, and expectations openly. Regular check-ins and discussions help ensure that all parties are aligned and comfortable with the relationship dynamics.

   - **Negotiating Boundaries**: Establishing and negotiating boundaries is crucial for maintaining intimacy. Boundaries may include agreements about sexual health, emotional involvement, and time management. Respecting these boundaries fosters trust and mutual respect.

2. **Cultivating Trust**:
   - **Transparency and Honesty**: Transparency about interactions with other partners and honesty about feelings and experiences are vital for building and maintaining trust. Keeping partners informed and involved helps prevent misunderstandings and fosters a secure environment.

   - **Managing Jealousy**: Jealousy is a common issue in ENM relationships. Addressing jealousy through open communication, self-reflection, and support from partners helps manage and overcome these feelings. Recognizing and addressing underlying insecurities can also contribute to a healthier relationship dynamic.

3. **Fostering Emotional Connection**:
   - **Quality Time**: Spending quality time with each partner helps maintain and deepen emotional connections. Prioritizing individual relationships and making time for meaningful interactions supports intimacy.

   - **Emotional Support**: Providing emotional support to partners and seeking support in return is crucial for maintaining intimacy. Acknowledging and validating each other's feelings and experiences strengthens the bond between partners.

## Navigating Dynamics of Multiple Relationships

1. **Balancing Time and Energy**:
   - **Effective Time Management**: Managing

time and energy among multiple partners requires effective planning and organization. Creating schedules, setting priorities, and being mindful of each partner's needs helps maintain balance and prevent feelings of neglect.

- **Avoiding Burnout**: Balancing multiple relationships can be demanding. Avoiding burnout involves setting realistic expectations, practicing self-care, and ensuring that all partners receive adequate attention and support.

2. **Maintaining Relationship Health**:
   - **Regular Check-Ins**: Regular check-ins with each partner provide opportunities to discuss concerns, update agreements, and address any issues. These discussions help ensure that all parties feel heard and valued.
   - **Addressing Conflict**: Conflicts are natural in any relationship, including ENM. Addressing conflicts constructively involves open communication, active listening, and a willingness to compromise. Seeking resolution and understanding helps maintain healthy and supportive relationships.

## Ethical Considerations and Social Context

1. **Ethical Behavior**:
   - **Informed Consent**: Ensuring that all parties are fully informed and consenting is a fundamental aspect of ENM. Ethical behavior involves respecting agreements, honoring commitments, and acting with integrity.

- **Respecting Privacy**: Respecting the privacy of partners and maintaining confidentiality is crucial for ethical practice. Boundaries regarding personal information and interactions with others should be honored.

2. **Navigating Social Stigma**:
   - **Handling Judgment**: ENM relationships may face societal judgment or misunderstanding. Handling stigma involves educating others about ENM, advocating for acceptance, and finding supportive communities.

   - **Promoting Inclusivity**: Advocating for inclusivity and acceptance of diverse relationship structures helps foster a more understanding and supportive social environment. Sharing experiences and promoting positive representations of ENM can contribute to greater acceptance.

## Developing Skills for ENM Success

1. **Enhancing Communication Skills**:
   - **Active Listening**: Practicing active listening involves fully engaging with what partners are saying, validating their feelings, and responding thoughtfully. Effective listening strengthens communication and connection.

   - **Expressing Needs and Desires**: Clearly expressing needs, desires, and concerns helps ensure that all partners are aware of each other's expectations. Open expression fosters mutual understanding and support.

2. **Building Emotional Resilience**:
   - **Self-Awareness**: Developing self-awareness

helps individuals understand their own needs, triggers, and emotional responses. Self-awareness supports healthier interactions and greater emotional resilience.

○ **Seeking Support**: Seeking support from therapists, support groups, or trusted friends can provide valuable insights and assistance. Support networks help individuals navigate the complexities of ENM and maintain well-being.

## Conclusion

Ethical non-monogamy offers a unique framework for intimacy that emphasizes consensual and transparent relationships with multiple partners. Building and maintaining intimacy in ENM requires clear communication, trust, and mutual respect. By addressing challenges, fostering emotional connections, and navigating the dynamics of multiple relationships, individuals can create fulfilling and meaningful connections. Understanding ethical considerations and social contexts further supports the development of healthy and supportive ENM relationships. In the next chapter, we will explore the role of intimacy in fostering personal growth, focusing on how relational dynamics contribute to individual development and well-being.

# CHAPTER 48: EXPLORING SENSUAL INTIMACY

Sensual intimacy goes beyond mere physical or emotional closeness, encompassing the full spectrum of sensory experiences to enhance connection and pleasure. It involves engaging the senses—touch, sight, sound, taste, and smell—to foster deeper connections and enrich intimate relationships. This chapter explores the role of sensuality in enhancing intimacy, offering practical tips and exercises to deepen sensual connections and create more fulfilling experiences.

**Understanding Sensual Intimacy**

1. **Defining Sensual Intimacy**:
   - **Sensuality vs. Sexuality**: Sensual intimacy focuses on engaging the senses to enhance pleasure and connection without necessarily involving sexual activity. It encompasses activities that stimulate the senses, such as touch, scent, sound, and taste, to foster a deeper sense of closeness and enjoyment.

   - **Role in Relationships**: Sensual intimacy plays a significant role in enhancing emotional and physical bonds. By focusing on sensory experiences, partners can create moments of joy, relaxation, and connection that strengthen their relationship.

2. **The Benefits of Sensual Intimacy**:
   - **Enhanced Connection**: Engaging the senses helps partners connect on a deeper level, fostering a greater sense of closeness and understanding. Sensual experiences can create lasting memories and deepen emotional bonds.
   - **Increased Pleasure**: Sensual activities can enhance pleasure and satisfaction, contributing to a more fulfilling relationship. By focusing on sensory experiences, partners can explore new dimensions of pleasure and enjoyment.

**Engaging the Senses**

1. **Touch**:
   - **The Power of Touch**: Touch is a fundamental aspect of sensual intimacy. It can range from gentle caresses and massages to playful touches and more intimate gestures. The power of touch lies in its ability to convey warmth, affection, and connection.
   - **Techniques for Deepening Touch**: Explore different types of touch to enhance intimacy. Techniques include giving and receiving massages, holding hands, and using different textures and temperatures to stimulate the skin.

2. **Sight**:
   - **Visual Stimulation**: Visual experiences can enhance sensual intimacy by creating a stimulating environment. This can include appreciating each other's appearance, using

lighting to set a mood, or engaging in visual activities such as watching romantic films or creating art together.

- **Enhancing Visual Connection**: Focus on visual aspects that evoke positive emotions. This might involve dressing in a way that pleases your partner, setting up a visually appealing space, or sharing moments that highlight each other's beauty.

3. **Sound**:

- **Auditory Experiences**: Sound plays a significant role in sensual intimacy. This includes the sounds of a partner's voice, music that creates a romantic atmosphere, or soothing background noise that promotes relaxation.

- **Creating a Soundscape**: Use music, nature sounds, or other auditory elements to enhance the sensory experience. Creating a personalized soundscape can set the mood and enhance the overall connection.

4. **Taste**:

- **Exploring Flavors**: Taste can enhance sensual intimacy through shared culinary experiences. This can involve cooking together, savoring a meal, or exploring new flavors and textures.

- **Sensory Eating**: Pay attention to the experience of eating together. Focus on the flavors, textures, and aromas of the food, and use this opportunity to connect and share enjoyment.

5. **Smell**:

- **Olfactory Stimulation**: Smell has a

powerful effect on emotional and sensory experiences. Aromas can evoke memories, create a calming environment, or enhance relaxation.

- **Using Scents**: Incorporate pleasant scents into your relationship, such as through aromatherapy, scented candles, or perfumes. Choose scents that are enjoyable and calming for both partners.

**Practical Tips for Deepening Sensual Intimacy**

1. **Set the Mood**:
   - **Creating Atmosphere**: Establish a sensual atmosphere by setting up a space that appeals to the senses. Use soft lighting, calming music, and comfortable textures to create an inviting environment.
   - **Intentional Moments**: Designate specific times for sensual experiences, such as a weekly date night or a special occasion. Intentional moments help prioritize and cultivate sensual intimacy.

2. **Explore New Sensory Activities**:
   - **Sensory Exploration**: Try new activities that engage the senses. This might include trying new foods, exploring different types of touch, or experimenting with new sensory experiences together.
   - **Creative Outlets**: Engage in creative activities that stimulate the senses, such as painting, dancing, or crafting. Creative experiences can enhance sensual intimacy by providing opportunities for connection and self-expression.

3. **Communicate and Listen**:
   - **Discuss Preferences**: Openly communicate with your partner about sensory preferences and desires. Discuss what types of touch, sights, sounds, tastes, and smells are most enjoyable for both of you.
   - **Active Listening**: Pay attention to your partner's feedback and preferences. Actively listen to their responses and adjust sensory experiences to meet their needs and desires.

4. **Practice Mindfulness**:
   - **Being Present**: Practice mindfulness to fully engage in sensory experiences. Focus on the present moment and savor each sensation without distractions or judgment.
   - **Mindful Touch**: Practice mindful touch by paying attention to the sensations and responses of your partner. Use touch as a way to connect and communicate affection.

**Enhancing Sensual Intimacy Through Exploration**

1. **Engage in Sensory Play**:
   - **Playful Exploration**: Incorporate sensory play into your relationship to enhance intimacy. This might include playful activities such as sensory games, exploration of different textures, or experimenting with new sensations.
   - **Mutual Discovery**: Use sensory play as an opportunity for mutual discovery and connection. Explore each other's preferences and enjoy the process of learning and growing together.

2. **Create Rituals and Traditions**:

- **Sensual Rituals**: Establish rituals or traditions that involve sensory experiences. This could include regular massages, shared meals, or sensory-focused activities that you both enjoy.

- **Building Connection**: Rituals and traditions create opportunities for regular connection and intimacy. They provide a framework for nurturing and maintaining sensual experiences.

## Conclusion

Sensual intimacy enriches relationships by engaging the senses to foster connection and pleasure. By understanding and exploring the role of touch, sight, sound, taste, and smell, partners can deepen their connection and enhance their experiences together. Implementing practical tips, exploring new sensory activities, and prioritizing communication and mindfulness can help cultivate a more fulfilling and intimate relationship. As we move forward in this book, the next chapter will delve into the intersection of intimacy and personal boundaries, examining how to navigate and respect individual limits while fostering connection.

# CHAPTER 49:
# THE JOURNEY OF LIFELONG INTIMACY

Lifelong intimacy is a dynamic and evolving process that requires ongoing effort, adaptability, and commitment. It involves nurturing and sustaining deep connections through the various stages of life, facing challenges, celebrating successes, and continuously growing together. This chapter explores the journey of maintaining intimacy over the long term, emphasizing the importance of adaptability, communication, and mutual support.

**Understanding Lifelong Intimacy**

1. **The Nature of Lifelong Intimacy**:
    - **Continuous Growth**: Lifelong intimacy is characterized by continuous growth and adaptation. Relationships evolve as individuals and circumstances change, requiring partners to adapt and respond to new challenges and opportunities.

    - **Deepening Connection**: Over time, intimacy can deepen as partners develop a greater understanding of each other and build a shared history. Lifelong intimacy involves growing closer through shared experiences, mutual support, and ongoing communication.

2. **Key Components of Lifelong Intimacy**:
    - **Adaptability**: The ability to adapt to changes and challenges is crucial for maintaining intimacy over time. Relationships face various transitions, such as career changes, health issues, and family dynamics, requiring partners to remain flexible and supportive.

    - **Communication**: Effective communication is essential for addressing issues, expressing needs, and maintaining a strong connection. Lifelong intimacy requires ongoing dialogue and openness to navigate the complexities of long-term relationships.

    - **Mutual Support**: Supporting each other through life's ups and downs strengthens the bond of intimacy. Providing emotional, practical, and moral support helps partners navigate challenges and celebrate achievements together.

## Strategies for Nurturing Lifelong Intimacy

1. **Embrace Change**:
    - **Adapting to Life Stages**: Recognize that intimacy evolves as individuals progress through different life stages. Embrace changes in roles, responsibilities, and priorities, and find ways to adapt your relationship to new circumstances.

    - **Flexibility and Growth**: Be open to change and growth within the relationship. Flexibility allows partners to navigate challenges and seize opportunities for deeper connection and understanding.

2. **Foster Effective Communication**:

- **Regular Check-Ins**: Schedule regular check-ins to discuss feelings, needs, and concerns. Regular communication helps address issues before they escalate and ensures that both partners feel heard and valued.

- **Active Listening**: Practice active listening to understand your partner's perspective. Show empathy and validation, and work together to find solutions to any challenges that arise.

3. **Celebrate Milestones and Achievements**:
   - **Marking Special Moments**: Celebrate milestones and achievements, such as anniversaries, personal accomplishments, and shared experiences. Recognizing and honoring these moments strengthens the bond of intimacy and creates lasting memories.

   - **Creating Traditions**: Establish traditions and rituals that celebrate your relationship and its journey. These can include annual events, special date nights, or personal rituals that reinforce your connection.

4. **Prioritize Quality Time**:
   - **Spending Time Together**: Make time for each other amidst the busyness of life. Prioritize quality time through activities that you both enjoy, such as hobbies, travel, or simply spending time together.

   - **Balancing Responsibilities**: Balance individual responsibilities and relationship priorities. Ensure that both partners have time to focus on the relationship, even amidst busy schedules and life demands.

5. **Maintain Physical and Emotional Connection**:
   - **Physical Affection**: Continue to express physical affection through touch, cuddling, and intimacy. Physical connection helps reinforce emotional bonds and contributes to overall relationship satisfaction.
   - **Emotional Intimacy**: Foster emotional intimacy by sharing thoughts, feelings, and experiences. Support each other's emotional well-being and maintain a deep connection through mutual understanding and empathy.

6. **Work Through Challenges Together**:
   - **Facing Difficulties**: Address challenges and conflicts as a team. Approach difficulties with a problem-solving mindset and work together to find solutions that strengthen the relationship.
   - **Seeking Support**: When facing significant challenges, consider seeking external support, such as counseling or therapy. Professional guidance can provide valuable tools and strategies for navigating complex issues.

## The Role of Adaptability in Lifelong Intimacy

1. **Embracing Life Transitions**:
   - **Navigating Change**: Life transitions, such as career changes, health issues, or family dynamics, can impact intimacy. Embrace these transitions as opportunities for growth and adaptation within the relationship.
   - **Supporting Each Other**: Provide mutual support during life transitions. Be

understanding and patient as your partner navigates changes, and work together to adjust and maintain intimacy.

2. **Evolving Relationship Dynamics**:
   - **Adapting to Growth**: As individuals grow and change, relationships must also evolve. Embrace each other's growth and adapt to new interests, goals, and experiences.
   - **Rediscovering Connection**: Regularly revisit and rediscover aspects of your relationship that may have changed. This helps maintain a sense of connection and ensures that the relationship continues to meet both partners' needs.

## Building a Lasting Connection

1. **Cultivate Shared Interests**:
   - **Pursuing Common Goals**: Engage in activities and interests that you both enjoy. Shared experiences create opportunities for connection and reinforce the bond of intimacy.
   - **Exploring New Interests**: Explore new interests and hobbies together. Trying new things can bring excitement to the relationship and provide opportunities for growth and discovery.

2. **Nurture Emotional Resilience**:
   - **Building Resilience**: Develop emotional resilience by supporting each other through challenges and setbacks. Strengthen your relationship by facing difficulties together and maintaining a positive outlook.
   - **Encouraging Personal Growth**: Support

each other's personal growth and development. Encourage individual pursuits and achievements, and celebrate successes together.

## Conclusion

The journey of lifelong intimacy requires ongoing effort, adaptability, and commitment. By embracing change, fostering effective communication, celebrating milestones, and maintaining physical and emotional connection, partners can nurture and sustain their relationship over time. Lifelong intimacy is a dynamic and evolving process that involves continuous growth and mutual support. As we conclude this exploration of intimacy, the next chapter will focus on practical exercises and techniques for integrating and applying the principles discussed throughout the book, helping readers to cultivate and enhance their intimate connections.

# CHAPTER 50: CONCLUSION: EMBRACING INTIMACY

As we reach the final chapter of this exploration into intimacy, it is fitting to reflect on the journey we've undertaken and the profound insights we've gained. Embracing intimacy in all its forms enriches our lives, deepens our relationships, and contributes to our overall well-being. This concluding chapter summarizes the key insights from the book, encouraging readers to fully embrace and cultivate intimacy in their personal and relational lives.

**The Essence of Intimacy**

Intimacy, at its core, is about forging deep, meaningful connections with others. It involves a blend of emotional, physical, and psychological closeness that transcends superficial interactions. Intimacy is not a static state but a dynamic process that evolves and grows over time. It requires ongoing effort, adaptability, and a willingness to be vulnerable.

**Key Insights from the Book**

1. **Emotional Intimacy**:
    - Emotional intimacy is the foundation of strong relationships, built on trust,

understanding, and mutual respect. Sharing thoughts, feelings, and experiences fosters a deep bond that enhances overall well-being.

2. **Physical Intimacy**:
   - Physical intimacy encompasses both sexual and non-sexual touch, such as hugging and holding hands. It plays a crucial role in strengthening relationships and expressing affection.

3. **Building Trust**:
   - Trust is a cornerstone of intimacy. Building and maintaining trust involves transparency, consistency, and reliability. Addressing and overcoming challenges together strengthens this vital aspect of relationships.

4. **Effective Communication**:
   - Open and honest communication is essential for developing and sustaining intimacy. It helps resolve conflicts, express needs, and deepen connections. Active listening and empathy are key components of effective communication.

5. **Intimacy in Different Relationships**:
   - Intimacy extends beyond romantic relationships to friendships, family, and professional interactions. Each type of relationship requires its own approach to building and maintaining intimacy.

6. **Navigating Challenges**:
   - Intimacy can be challenged by various factors, including trauma, conflict, and life transitions. Addressing these challenges with empathy, resilience, and

a commitment to growth is crucial for maintaining deep connections.

7. **The Role of Technology and Culture**:
   - Technology and cultural perspectives influence how we experience and express intimacy. Understanding these influences helps navigate modern relationships and embrace diverse forms of connection.

8. **Personal Growth and Self-Discovery**:
   - Personal growth and self-awareness enhance intimacy by fostering emotional intelligence and resilience. Engaging in self-discovery supports healthier and more fulfilling relationships.

9. **Lifelong Intimacy**:
   - Maintaining intimacy over the long term involves adaptability, celebration of milestones, and consistent effort. Lifelong intimacy requires nurturing and evolving with each other through various life stages.

## Embracing Intimacy

Embracing intimacy means recognizing its profound impact on our lives and actively nurturing it. Here are some ways to fully embrace and integrate intimacy into your daily life:

1. **Be Present and Engaged**:
   - Fully engage in your relationships by being present and attentive. Prioritize quality time and meaningful interactions to strengthen connections.

2. **Practice Vulnerability**:
   - Allow yourself to be vulnerable and open with others. Sharing your true self fosters deeper connections and builds trust.

3. **Foster Empathy and Understanding**:
    - Cultivate empathy by actively listening and seeking to understand others' perspectives. Show compassion and support to deepen emotional bonds.

4. **Communicate Openly and Honestly**:
    - Practice clear and honest communication. Address issues promptly and work together to resolve conflicts and strengthen your relationship.

5. **Celebrate and Nurture Relationships**:
    - Celebrate milestones, achievements, and special moments with your loved ones. Regularly nurture your relationships through small gestures and acts of affection.

6. **Adapt and Grow Together**:
    - Embrace change and growth within your relationships. Adapt to new circumstances and continue to support each other through life's transitions.

7. **Seek Support When Needed**:
    - Don't hesitate to seek external support if needed. Therapy and counseling can provide valuable tools and strategies for improving and sustaining intimacy.

8. **Integrate Intimacy into Daily Life**:
    - Incorporate intimacy into your daily routines and interactions. Small acts of love and appreciation contribute to a stronger and more fulfilling connection.

## The Value of Intimacy

Intimacy enhances personal growth, emotional well-being, and overall life satisfaction. It provides a sense of connection, support, and understanding that enriches our lives and relationships. By embracing intimacy, we open ourselves to deeper connections, greater joy, and a more meaningful existence.

As you move forward, remember that intimacy is a journey, not a destination. It requires ongoing effort, adaptability, and a genuine commitment to nurturing and growing your relationships. Embrace intimacy with an open heart and mind, and allow it to enrich every aspect of your life.

Thank you for joining me on this exploration of intimacy. May the insights and practices shared throughout this book guide you in cultivating and sustaining deep, meaningful connections that bring joy, fulfillment, and resilience to your life.

## Thank You Message

Dear Readers,

Thank you for embarking on this journey with me through *Intimacy Unveiled: Exploring the Depths of Human Connection.* It has been a profound privilege to share these insights on intimacy and human connection with you. Your engagement and dedication to understanding the complexities of intimacy inspire me, and I am deeply grateful for your support.

Writing this book has been an enriching experience, and I hope that the concepts, strategies, and reflections within these pages have resonated with you and provided valuable perspectives. Intimacy is a vital aspect of our lives, and exploring its many facets—emotional, physical, and psychological—offers us the opportunity to deepen our relationships and enhance our overall well-being.

Whether you have sought to improve your romantic relationships, strengthen your friendships, or better understand yourself, I hope this book has been a helpful guide in your quest for deeper connections. Remember that intimacy is a continuous journey, and each step you take towards understanding and embracing it brings you closer to a more fulfilling and meaningful life.

As you continue to explore and nurture the intimate relationships in your life, I encourage you to carry forward the lessons and insights shared in this book. Embrace vulnerability, practice empathy, and communicate openly. By doing so, you contribute to the creation of stronger, more resilient connections that enrich your life and the lives of those around you.

Thank you once again for your trust and for allowing me to be a part of your journey towards greater intimacy. Your commitment to fostering deeper connections is truly inspiring, and I am honored to have been a part of your exploration.

With heartfelt gratitude,

Raj Kishor Mahapatra